From Invisible
to Incredible

From Invisible to Incredible

THE SECRET TO BRILLIANT EXECUTIVE PRESENCE

Angela Marie Nuttle

ISBN: 1514729253
ISBN 13: 9781514729250
Library of Congress Control Number: 2015910454
CreateSpace Independent Publishing Platform
North Charleston, South Carolina

*To Mackenzie Nuttle, who inspired me by doing cartwheels
In the living room as I wrote this book.*

She is the future poster child of executive presence.

Table of Contents

Dear Reader,

*A*s a corporate talent expert, I am frequently asked this question:

"What is it that causes talented people not to be seen, heard, or recognized for their actual value?" Here's the most common answer I receive from executives and business leaders:

"It's the absence of authentic executive presence."

This book is powerful for 4 types of people in business, all with unique perspectives:

Individuals: You're the high performer trying to make your mark, or an aspiring leader wanting to grow in the company. You could also be the seasoned expert longing to be respected in your craft. You've tried to prove yourself, but can't seem to break through to that executive level. You may feel like you're operating below your calling and potential. Read and apply this book.

Executives: You are busy and your schedule is tough. You don't have visibility of all the talent in your organization, and many people who get on your calendar don't know how to engage with you in a memorable way. When your agenda is filled with back-to-back presentations, you just wish someone would teach them how to show up strong. This book will help you understand their struggles, their value, and how they can overcome. Give this book to them, to your managers, and to your HR team.

Managers: You are trying to figure out how to help your talented employees become successful. Growing them reflects on your leadership ability. Their results are your results and you want to help them demonstrate their worth. You also have aspirations for your own career. Read this book and use it to help your team elevate their performance and careers.

HR Professionals: You are responsible for the overall development of talent. You work with everyone and are trying to figure out how to get everyone connected. You want to develop people with the right skills to build the company. If you're successful at this, you'll gain credibility as a trusted advisor. Use this book to start developing your organization, but also yourself because you are often in front of leadership representing your craft.

Enjoy the book!

Introduction

$\mathcal{W}$e begin with a personal war.

A battlefield of questions furiously worked inside me: Do I really think I can walk in, command the room, establish myself as an expert in my field, and come out of there as a trusted advisor? My goal was to show the value of our work to the rest of the organization, and gain respect as a thought leader. Would I be courageous enough to defend my highly thought out plan and hold their attention long enough to avoid a presentation hijack?

I shuddered at the thought of others in this same position, trying to fight off the knee jerk reactions of busy executives. Few people were successful in winning the hearts and minds in this elite room where it could get dangerous in a hurry. Smart people with solid data walked out devastated. They were transformed into subservient victims whose good work was minimized, rearranged, or tossed out. I needed a source of courage because I felt like I was walking into a war zone.

Nervousness had arrived. In 5 minutes, I would be presenting on a key program to top executives of a multi-billion dollar Fortune 500 company. My division vice president invited me to the quarterly corporate executive meeting to show off our work and was expecting a great performance. This was a critical moment in my career with high stakes...

You have your own version of this story. You've found yourself at a pivotal moment that could possibly determine your future. This could be the experience that elevates your credibility and career. Finally, everyone will see your potential! Or will they?

Your mind is racing as fast as your heart. Fear sets in. What if you forget something or you stumble? What if you don't know the answer to an important question, and you are humiliated in front of the top leaders in the company? What if they don't see the real you, an important person with ideas and results who deserves recognition—and respect?

Meanwhile, inside the boardroom, the atmosphere is palpable. The tension, combined with exhaustion from the earlier strategy discussion, has all executives on edge. The conversation has been vacated at a critical time so everything can stay on schedule. The presentations so far have been boring, overloaded with ridiculous details, and unremarkable. There's one last *agenda item*—a presenter—and then everyone can get back to the real problems. This better be good—and quick.

It feels as though an invisible gatekeeper has shown up whose goal is to keep all parties from getting in sync. You're sitting outside the room, contemplating how to connect with these top-level leaders. You have brilliant ideas, knowledge, and revelations to share. At the same time, *they* are bombarded with business challenges, agendas, and mind-numbing presentations that leave them frustrated and downright sharp-tongued.

Even though you get a chance to enter the room physically, you may end up walking away without being seen, heard, or celebrated for your value. Will you be left to continue operating below your calling and capability? Where does your mind go in this precarious moment?

My mind instantly went to Iraq. I spent three years there, dodging enemy attacks while trying to help my company support the US military. In 2004, I boarded a C-31 plane headed for a warzone as a defense contractor. I would be helping Marines and soldiers transition into and out of the war environment, but my permanent role would evolve to human resources leadership on the base. Early on, female contractors were few in number. All 16 of us were surrounded by hundreds of male Marines and contractors undergoing some of the most character defining moments of our lives.

The air was a sweltering 120 degrees. It was a miserable experience to wear 50-pound protective gear everywhere I went. The mode of transportation in this sandpit was two blistered feet in unbelievably tight, sweaty boots, which made the long walk to the chow hall excruciating. My only motivation was food.

Sometimes the food truck would make it into the base, and we would get a nice greasy buffet of "stuff", but it was more likely that the truck wouldn't show. Our alternative was an MRE (Meal Ready to Eat)—not quite the fine dining experience I was imagining on that long walk! The first 30 days were intense and difficult.

You'd think the most frightening part of the whole situation was the actual war, but it wasn't. Everyone was there by choice, and we were trained to follow a strict protocol that kept us safe. Bombings and explosions could be heard all around the base, and we learned to hit the prone position if anything sounded close. If our base was under attack with rockets and mortars in the air, we headed to the nearest bunker. Besides, I had a spiritual sense of assurance that we were protected.

The toughest part of being there was the hostility toward women from many of the male contractors early in my deployment. A "wild west" mentality existed amongst the gentlemen, and the treatment of females was shocking! In fact, several went home because they couldn't withstand the situation. It was clear that I was not welcome in their boys' club. I found myself a target for antagonistic verbal abuse, angry threats, and stalking. I managed to maintain my composure and treated everyone with respect, although I was highly intimidated. I did a lot of praying.

Being in a war zone with people who either want to kill you or want you gone really puts life into perspective. I obviously survived. I learned who I was and what my character looked like in times of trouble (which wasn't always perfect). The fruit that it produced overshadowed the tougher memories, and I developed tremendous social intelligence and resilience.

Now I was facing a different kind of "war" as I prepared to enter a boardroom in heels instead of steel-toed boots. There would be no MREs or greasy buffets. I planned to deliver a "fine dining" experience and win the respect of each person there. Yes, I had earned my right to be there.

My 5 minutes of soul searching were up and it was time to go in for the presentation. I felt confident as I entered the room where a multitude of leaders were engaging in serious conversations. They weren't aware of me as I joined them, which was an opportunity for me to take a deep breath while I scoped out the place. It would take a compelling opener to get their attention...

That moment of entering the room is surreal. You have to know with certainty that you deserve to be in the room. You have a valuable contribution to make to the mission, and it's time to share that. The room appears to be a battlefield, or even a stage, but you rise above that by remaining calm, focused, and authentic. You've been planning your strategy for a while now, and determination won't allow you to get caught up in skirmishes that lead to dead ends. You've trained yourself through life experiences to stand courageously in this moment, and it's time to *show up ... as you.*

Leaders are taking advantage of the transition between agenda items, trying to work through the last action item that the CEO issued. It's another hoop to jump, leaving everyone scurrying to adjust booked schedules and plans. Every minute is precious. If only one more decision could just be squeezed in before the next *agenda item*, which is walking in the door now.

The lights went down and a mesmerizing orchestra played in a short musical video created to grandly introduce the program. The bass tones vibrated in the chests of everyone in the room, and they instantly stopped their chatter to look at the brilliant images on the screen. I had their full attention now, and, as the video came to an end, I moved to the center of the room, stepping in close to the group.

"[This program] is dramatically changing the way our division is doing business. Our customer knows it; our people love it, and our bottom line business results show it! I'm your program manager who is supporting this mission. I am going to tell you what this program is, and how

its impact has contributed to saving a multi-million dollar contract that was in danger of being lost..."

You have their attention, and you nail it. What an overwhelming feeling of triumph, and relief! You see the looks on their faces, and they are not thinking about whatever it was they were discussing before. They are looking at you. Some look surprised, others are scrunching their foreheads in deep thought, and yet others are smiling with excitement and curiosity. You are in the process of being seen, heard, and respected.

What's this person's name? Which division is she in? How does this program work? What can we do to save more contracts and get people engaged? The people in the room are suddenly focused and want to know more. You've prepared thoroughly for this time. You know the data, you've run through the possible objections and you're showing up comfortably in your own skin. Of course, a couple of executives have to poke at you a bit, testing your preparation, but you respectfully counter. In that moment you move from *invisible to incredible*. You are a bright bulb in the room and it feels good...

HOW DO YOU GET HERE?

How do you learn to show up with authentic executive presence, and what does that even mean? You may be wrestling with a few thoughts or experiences that keep you from envisioning your brilliance in this scenario:

- You've been traumatized by a meeting/presentation experience gone wrong

- You've been told you need to develop *presence* or work on your presentation skills in order to move up
- You've never been given feedback on how you show up, which tells you something
- You are simply motivated to grow and develop your career, now you just need to figure out what to do

Everything in this book is based upon recent research, coupled with many years of corporate experience, observation, and the results of learning experiments. The truth of the matter is that there are two parties involved in the determination of executive presence: your audience and you. Although you can't control other people, you can learn to manage them effectively. Your main focus will be working on the things that you can control, which include your behavior, emotional responses, and level of expertise.

I will help you crack the code to get past that imaginary gatekeeper that keeps you from being successful. You'll learn the secrets of breaking through to that next level while getting some critical tools you need to discover and develop your value. The goal is to showcase your worth, and I like to call this: ***Showing up—you!***

I've coached many aspiring leaders, high performers, and high potential people, like you, to shine in their current roles then move on to their next level of career success. I've also partnered with executive leaders and HR experts to develop and *remodel* talented individuals so they can effectively support a greater mission in the company—and in life.

At a very fundamental level, I've been in your shoes and learned how NOT to be humiliated in front of top organizational leaders in meetings and in presentations. I want to help you overcome the fear that eats you up and prevents you from thriving.

You'll also improve your ability to engage people through authenticity, confidence, and social agility. Others will start to recognize and appreciate your personal and professional value. However, there is one caveat: you have to be willing to do the work.

Executives, your struggles involve making the most effective use of your time while discovering and developing your talent to meet the business objectives. You don't have time to waste, and you are looking for succinct information and powerful encounters. You see lots of people every day and it gets blurry, so it is harder to see the value of your existing talent because you may not even know who and what you have. You are most likely losing profitability because you don't have visibility and you are struggling to valuate people properly. This book is designed to be an advocate for you, but it's also made to help the people who come in contact with you to perform and interact at a higher level so you can truly understand the goldmine you have available to you. You have a big role assessing talent in a way that allows the business to prosper. You have a greater purpose of courageously caring about the people carrying your vision.

HR professionals and people managers, we'll go deeper than just constructing a PowerPoint and wearing the right clothes. Although executive presence and executive presentation are two separate entities, there's an interesting relationship that we will explore. You'll discover how to help activate the individual's gift of presence, while learning the "what and how" of executive presentation. This book is designed to speak to you. You desire to be a trusted advisor to the business, and there's something here for you as well.

We'll work through a practical method called "The Fine Dining Delivery Experience"™, which puts the spotlight on each person's unique style for audiences from one to ten thousand. I want you to learn how to be seen, heard, and valued. Most importantly, I want you to awaken your gift of presence. It's time to **SHOW UP YOU.**

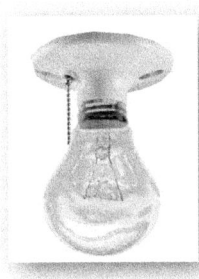

PART I

Executive Presence

THE REAL DEFINITION

What do you believe executive presence is? It seems that the definition is a mystery. The truth is that there's no official definition, so my intention is to help you shape it and start living it because it looks different to everyone.

Let's set the stage properly with recent study findings by Gavin Dagley and Caderyn Gaskin, whose work is cited in the APA (American Psychological Association) September 2014 Consulting Psychological Journal. Their research reveals this:

1. Executive presence is based on *audience perceptions* of a person's characteristics.
2. 10 core characteristics affect presence, and they are split in half for a two-part determination of executive presence.
3. *First impressions* are determined by perceptions around the first 5 (status/reputation, physical appearance, projected confidence, communication ability, engagement skills).
4. *Longer-term evaluation* is determined by the last 5 characteristics (interpersonal integrity, values in action, intelligence/expertise, outcome delivery ability, coercive power use).

I would distill their research down to these important points:

- The 5 impression-based characteristics are more closely related to *career success*
- The 5 evaluation-based characteristics are more closely related to *organizational success*

- *Values in action* is the highest influencing factor of all characteristics
- Executive presence involves managing perceptions and exerting influence without formal authority while continuing to evolve personally over time

You may be asking yourself, "Do I have it?" If you are a human being with breath, you have some type of presence. "Yeah, but do I have EXECUTIVE presence?" When you look up the definition of "executive", here's what pops up:

"Having the power to put plans, actions, or laws into effect."

You may or may not be able to put actual laws into effect, but you are a human being who has the *power* to put *plans* and *actions* in place. You do that every day. You can embrace that power or you can deny it.

Traditional experts believe that executive presence means taking command of a room while capturing the attention of people and creating sophisticated conversation. I spoke with one person who was adamant that you couldn't wear a $19.99 sweater and have a *good look*. While those elements could certainly be some kind of sign, they focus on external attributes that don't fully capture the essence (or even come close). It's not always the flashy charismatic person with expensive clothing or the super intelligent James Bond type that magnetizes a room. People of all shapes, sizes, budgets, and mindsets have inspired people by simply being authentic.

Markku Kauppinen, CEO of Extended DISC North America, eloquently paints his picture of executive presence. *"The people I've seen demonstrate the highest level* of executive presence are those who have made peace with who they are. They're at peace with their strengths, as well as their needed areas of improvement."

That's powerful. Clearly, this is a process that starts on the inside of people versus the outside. We will work on the external factors, but we will also spend time figuring out how to make peace with who we really are. When we are at peace with ourselves, we are in alignment with our values, and we act consistently with them. Other people sense our inner calm and are drawn to its simplicity. This comes down to having a deeper YES living inside you that compels you to stand in courage. It also pushes you to be *authentic.* This is so important that I am including it in our working definition:

The power of an authentic human being to put plans and actions into effect.

Let's zoom in on HOW you can cultivate authenticity and draw people to your purpose.

Tip: *As you go through the book, circle words and key phrases that resonate with you. You may want to start making a list of them because you will be using it to create your unique definition of executive presence in Chapter 6.*

CHAPTER 1

The Choice of Authenticity

*W*e need to spend time focusing on some key ingredients of executive presence, like authenticity. Today's successful businessperson shows up as genuine and real. Tomorrow will bring 5 generations into the workplace for the first time ever, and the values of business are shifting to relationships, community, and authenticity. If you don't have this, your quest for a successful business career will be difficult and short-lived. It makes sense to know what the dictionary says about the word *"authentic"*. Here's what it says:

"*Of undisputed origin; genuine.*"

Naturally, dictionaries are seen as the authority of meaning. One thing is clear, a small number of people created dictionaries. You have the freedom to shape a more personal meaning. When *you* create it, it is of *undisputed origin and genuine.*

Take a moment to process how you would define authenticity and what it really means to you. What comes to mind?

Images of certain people may surface during your reflection. Their characteristics and mannerisms stand out, and we might even romanticize their personalities. I like what my friend Markku Kauppinen says about this. *"We tend to look for a hero and be them. People make the mistake of reflecting on who they want to be instead of who they really are."*

Concentrate on what YOU look like as authentic versus emulating someone else or comparing yourself.

I equate it to the world of art. When an artist creates art, it is an original piece. Anyone who paints a replica or makes a print of it is copying it. It's not original. The same principle applies to your authentic presence. You have a beautiful mural going on inside of you that is original and of undisputed origin. Don't copy someone else's art.

WHAT MAKES YOU REAL?

Your background has yielded deep convictions and beliefs that bring out the real you. These are uncompromising and part of your daily fabric. You can probably recall events that have led to the creation of *your personal mural, or authenticity.* Think about it. What's really important to you?

I have a belief that fun and laughter have a magical way of letting the real me breathe. My father brought this out in me and I considered him to be the king of hilariousness. His silly antics, although sometimes unpleasantly aromatic, caused me to abandon all poise and double over with uncontrollable, teary-eyed laughter! Those experiences developed my great appreciation for humor, and I learned to pass that joy along (except for the unpleasant aromatic part!).

Laughter and joy are good ways to get *the gatekeeper* out of the way. We fear them because they make us vulnerable, but laughing or expressing your joy can be the quickest way to break down the barrier between you and the room. The key is that your output has to be *real*.

SQUASHED AUTHENTICITY

How do you handle it when someone infringes upon your beliefs?

When you feel like your core values are being challenged or threatened, it's a 100% normal reaction to protect yourself by withdrawing your authenticity. I call this *allowing yourself to get squashed*.

We learn to guard ourselves from vulnerability early in life, and we formulate beliefs that we have to squash who we really are and appear perfect. The pressure to design our lives to someone else's pattern becomes the bigger yes.

Why?

We don't want to risk discomfort or humiliation, and we truly fear being susceptible to rejection.

We want to fit in, so we allow others' voices to dictate how we show up. Their model becomes our definition of perfection. When we copy, it is never perfect. This is one reason why we never feel like we measure up. Others sense our insecurity, and it hurts our executive presence.

One summer, I went to a weeklong Pentecostal church camp with my Grandma Dixie. Imagine her surprise when she opened my suitcase to find bunch of cute little shorts and summer halter-tops that my mom packed. I didn't understand why wearing my own clothing was wrong, but Grandma Dixie managed to get me the *politically correct* attire to avoid my banishment from camp. The whole week was tough for me. I was the smallest camper there, I didn't know any of the kids—who happened to be older—and I wore their tent-size clothing. Talk about being uncomfortable! My belief was that I didn't fit in and it wasn't acceptable to be myself, a heavy introspection for a first grader to carry around.

I realized years later that I was measuring myself against the wrong definition, and that's why I didn't fit. I constantly battled with being unsure and second-guessing myself. I squashed so much of my true self because I didn't think the world would welcome me for who I was. When I saw that I was attributing the church camp experience to the rest of my life, I began creating and applying the right definition:

Perfection is about being authentic. Authenticity comes from within.

The closest you can come to worldly perfection is being your true self, and that's through the expression of your own *mural*, NOT copying someone else's art piece.

You may be struggling to synthesize this, so I'll ask a *to the point* question:

What prevents you from showing up with authority and credibility?

You want to fit. You think you have to fit into a certain mold to be seen and heard, so you've shut down your authenticity. My mission is to help you get free from this imprisoned mindset and move into your professional calling and full capability while still managing the impressions of others effectively.

HOW COMFORTABLE ARE YOU?

Have you ever thought about how fabulous it would be to live in total peace with all people, all the time—just by being yourself? It's definitely possible. You can move toward this goal by taking an honest look at your personal and professional life in terms of your comfort levels with varying groups of people.

You know when and how you show up as the real you. Let's explore your comfort levels through a 12-question self-assessment, which can be found on the next page. Think in terms of this rating scale:

A) ALWAYS
B) MOST TIMES
C) SOMETIMES
D) VERY LITTLE
E) NOT AT ALL

Remember, it is critically important that you be candid with yourself. Avoid the temptation to rationalize or defend yourself, just check the responses that best fit your situation. Once you answer, tally your results by adding the checkmarks then multiplying each column by the designated number. Finally, create the grand total at the bottom and review what your score indicates.

COMFORT LEVEL ASSESSMENT

I'm Comfortable with...	Always	Most Times	Some-times	Very Little	Not At All
Being alone					
Family at home					
Relatives					
Friends					
People I don't know very well					
My peers					
Other professionals					
My leader					
Other leaders					
Someone who opposes my view					
Being vulnerable					
Being different than others around me					
TOTAL # OF CHECKMARKS					
Multiply by the indicated amount	X5	X4	X3	X2	X1
TOTAL SCORES					
OVERALL TOTAL					

What your scores indicate:

50-60 Points: High Comfort

You have a great balance of authenticity in your personal and professional life. You are at peace with who you are. You typically remain consistent in your approach, no matter who is around. You may also be mentoring others who are drawn to you. It's not unusual for people to tell you that you come across as genuine and real. When you get feedback that is less than ideal for you, you don't get out of sorts. You take it, reflect, and do something because you want to be your best. You also recognize when to "chew up the meat and spit out the bones" when you get feedback. You have the opportunity to fine-tune your natural abilities and presence so you can be even more effective than you already are.

39-49 Points: Average Comfort

Most people who take this assessment fall into this category. Your audience is the primary driver of sharing your true self. In your personal life, you may show up with strong comfort, while in other areas, like your professional life, you tend to be reserved. Those closest to you get to experience the real you. You have a decent foundation to build upon. It's important that you work through the concepts in this book to discover your path to deeper self-awareness and courage.

12-38 Points: Low Comfort

You are most comfortable squashing the real you and tend to be guarded. Being vulnerable takes a significant amount of energy from you. You've likely had life experiences that have influenced your need for heightened security. You may struggle with trusting the people around you. You feel safe being yourself with few close contacts, but that doesn't happen often. Remember that you always live in choice. You will make progress when you choose to say YES to courage, and NO to isolation and guardedness.

YOUR PERSONAL AND PROFESSIONAL LIFE

The 12 questions you've responded to are related to your personal and professional life. Your personal life responses are the foundational piece of the assessment. If you score high on these questions, you have a great advantage in cultivating a higher level of authenticity faster than others. Of course, this all depends on how straightforward you were with your answers. Were you honest?

Here's something to chew on.

If you believe you're being yourself but you don't ever get feedback that supports it, there's probably a disconnect somewhere that you need to address.

My husband and I have chatted about this a few times, and he's adamant that guys don't tell other guys, "Hey, you are authentic." No worries. If this is the case for you, be bold and ask people how you show up to them. Take note of how they describe you and see if any of it coincides with being genuine.

Most people have lower scores on the professional life segment of the assessment, which is normal. Here's where you can make meaningful progress in your overall executive presence, and it will take *brutal* self-awareness mixed with courage.

You have to allow yourself the freedom to be genuine.

You are faced with a decision that will impact the rest of your work in this area. Ask yourself if you are willing to do these four things:

- ° Objectively look at your own behavior without making excuses
- ° Celebrate and build upon the ways you show up as the real you
- ° Recognize the times when you squash it
- ° Take courageous action to develop it in ways that are noticeable—to the point that others call it out
- ° Stop trying to FIT

A key word is *willing*. If you are willing to take these steps in the spirit of courage, you are ready to move forward.

I need to emphasize an important distinction between the freedom to be yourself versus the license to be a jerk.

Does your demeanor affect people in a positive or negative way? Being the real deal aligns with being true to your values, morals and beliefs, while representing those respectfully. It doesn't mean that you behave unprofessionally. I've heard people use their beliefs as an excuse to be oppositional and stubborn. "That's just how I roll," or "That's just who I am and you're going to have to get over it" are not emotionally intelligent ways to represent yourself.

It's you who has to change your mindset, not the people around you.

Keep this close to your heart as you work through the book. You have the power to shift the way you think, but you may not realize it yet. Sometimes it feels really good to stay in victim or blaming mode, but if you want to grow, it has to GO.

THE CHOICE OF ACTION

You've been on a scavenger hunt in search of puzzle pieces to the real you. Honor yourself now by *choosing* to take the right action. It's time for others to see you at your best.

What will you do with this challenge? You could choose to do nothing, and nothing will change. You could make a long laundry list of things you'll start doing better, but that's like making a new year's resolution. We all know how that ends up.

The way to succeed is to make a plan with 1-3 small actions around your authenticity that can be implemented gradually. These can include self-challenges, experiments, acts of courage, or behavior modification.

Think about what you want to be different about you a month from now.

Here are some idea-sparking questions to consider:

° What's one small way you can demonstrate genuineness for a day?
° Which trigger troubles you the most and how can you manage it?
° What's the most courageous thing you can do to be yourself in front of others?
° What's the one thing you can do to stop trying to fit in?

Once you land on a small number of actions you can take, write down what you are going to do. You don't have to have some type of fancy worksheet here, just jot them down in a journal or add them as calendar invites to remind yourself about them.

Look at accountability as a *non-negotiable*. Half of the plan is finding a way to ensure you own this process and are doing something meaningful. You may even consider allowing a close friend, mentor, or coach in on your actions, and have them check in with you. As you make progress (or even have setbacks), write them down and discuss them.

For those who need help with practical steps, here are a few examples for you:

° Deal with a person who triggers anger in you by creating a planned objective response such as, "I

appreciate your opinion," or "Let me think about what you are saying."
     ° Experiment with telling a personal story during a presentation or meeting that relates to the discussion topic
     ° Challenge yourself to honestly state your opinion once a week

The practice of being real, genuine, and transparent takes courage. Frankly, this is about living in a way that honors the things that are important in your world. True authenticity wins hearts, and it strengthens your power. Insincerity alienates everyone, and you become obsolete.

It comes down to the bigger yes within you: Living your own values, or living in fear.

In terms of ingredients, authenticity is extremely vital in the mix of executive presence. You can equate it to the yeast that causes bread to rise. Without it, your presence falls flat. Bake in the real you, and you will rise to a whole new level of business success. And that's a fact.

CHAPTER 2

The Real Way to Build Confidence

SPOTLIGHT: YOU DON'T HAVE TO HAVE AN MBA TO BE CONFIDENT

Jennifer Zinn, a high level strategic executive for a major pharma-diagnostics company, discusses her early struggles with confidence and how she overcame them.

"I trained as an opera singer for years and I've been a performer all my life. It energizes me to be in front of a crowd." Jennifer speaks with a spark of fire in her eyes as she reminisces about her days onstage. Now she's a reckoning force on the stage of corporate America as an

assertive businesswoman who's seen her share of skirmishes and emerged with confidence.

Jennifer's natural ability to think through strategy and engage people surfaced early in her business career as she gravitated toward healthcare. She developed a love relationship with patient care, but found herself questioning her professional value.

"Most people walk around thinking about what they don't have in the corporate world. I struggled with not having the MBA or biology degree. A background as an opera singer? How could I measure up to scientists and engineers?" Jennifer's resignation that she was beneath her colleagues caught the attention of her mentor, Ray.

"Ray helped me to face my mental hurdle of feeling less than others. He asked me why I wasn't proud of my background. He worked with me to outline my experiences in a way that I had never thought of. Ray ultimately helped me to get over my obstacle and let it go."

Now with a new lens on the situation, "It makes me unique!" Jennifer declares with confidence. "I look at things differently. I also put values first; they are the root of my authenticity. I've established what's negotiable, and what's non-negotiable in my career and life." And it's clear that Jennifer values being transparent and resiliently genuine. Those qualities have led to her success. And she is slowly getting back on stage, but this time she's singing a different tune, speaking from the experience of an opera singer turned executive to those who need to hear, "No MBA degree required."

Confidence breeds more confidence...

We are drawn to it. We make decisions based on a person's ability to create a sense of security and trust. Employers select the confident candidate for the job, even if another candidate is more qualified. The sales guy wins the business because he knows his product and reassures the buyer that his solution will work best. We don't question doctors because we're certain they have everything under control and know what they're doing.

...lack of it brings alienation.

Insecurity is a big turnoff. Most executives will tell you they aren't concerned about your reasons for self-doubt; they just want to know if you have relevant information that furthers a business purpose. When we bring our emotional baggage with us, people see it and lose faith in our ability to perform. Frankly, it's uncomfortable for them and for you. You can look good and make a good first impression all day long, but if you don't have confidence, you won't truly influence or gain buy-in.

You need a certain mix of ingredients to influence...

You + Confidence + Authenticity= Influence + Credibility

You have the ability to influence the decisions that are being made in the room. Your bargaining power is a matter of having the guts to show up as yourself and trust in the things you already know (or at least what you think you know). If you add these things together, you will have influence and credibility.

...and there's a certain mix you should avoid.

You + Insecurity + Pretending to be Someone Else = Backfire
No explanation needed.

A PERFECT BALANCE OF CONFIDENCE AND AUTHENTICITY

When your audience experiences you operating within the credibility ingredients, it motivates them to act because you have a recipe for inspiration.

Remember the last time you were moved so powerfully that you set out to make yourself a better person? You DID something about it because there was some unseen force lifting you up emotionally, and you were determined to make some important change. That person who spoke was inspiring and had such influence that it made you feel like you could solve world peace. Personally, I think of Jesus.

Consider the biblical accounts of Jesus. Every writer in the Bible was in overwhelming awe of His presence. He demonstrated the gentleness of a lamb and the assertiveness of a lion. People flocked to Him, yearning to hear His words. He spoke fluid truth with complete transparency, but also with authority. He loved so deeply, yet His anger was like a lightning strike.

There was a fearful admiration when Jesus boldly gave honest feedback to the Pharisees. His followers couldn't peel themselves away from Him, and His energy drew them like bees to honey. If we could be like Him, our outcomes in the boardroom and meetings would be dramatically different. He knew when to comfort and when to belt out a rebuke, but He also knew when to be silent.

SILENT CONFIDENCE

Quietness can be profound. If you are a big chatty cat, you're most likely hurting your credibility by talking too much. There's a distorted belief that the more words we cram in, the bigger the chance people will buy what we are selling. We repeat ourselves, finding new ways of explaining the same thought until we've beaten it to death, all because we believe the other person will eventually hear us and glean a new revelation.

One Sunday, my pastor stepped into his usual place in front of an expectant crowd to begin his message. Instead of the typical opening joke or story, he stood in silence.

He looked comfortably to his left for several seconds with a resolute look on his face. With smoothness, his focus shifted to the middle section of the congregation. Another chunk of eternal seconds passed as he held his gaze open and his mouth closed.

Finally, he turned his face to the right, and rested there forever. I was fascinated by his method of connecting with everyone, eye to eye. Just when the tension could not be maintained any longer, as indicated by puzzled looks and side-cocked heads, he broke it.

"Silence is awkward."

The entire room exhaled, laughing. The atmosphere instantly lightened. The pastor smiled, himself relieved. He went on to tie in his opening exercise to a relevant message about God's silence between the old and new testaments of the Bible. The moment was stunning and memorable.

Quiet confidence is optimized by balance.

I want to be clear that I'm not advocating silence because you don't want to draw unnecessary attention, or you don't think your message is important enough. Recognize that you deserve to be in the room and you have something important to say. I'm encouraging you to speak up and make your words count with a laser sharp focus. This means letting your presence speak for itself.

ARROGANCE CLOAKED IN HUMILITY

You've most likely witnessed arrogance and cockiness. It's annoying to hear someone overestimate his or her value and knowledge. When people self-exalt, it's a sign of insecurity.

I ran across a particular leader in a company who shamelessly took credit for performance turnarounds of employees he coached. Although two of them were already great workers, the leader repetitively touted, "[The employee] was able to get on track because of my coaching and my work with him. I'm so grateful for the chance to lead him." I equated this leader's behavior to arrogance cloaked in humility. He was overcompensating for a self-perceived deficiency. The need to be accepted and validated was so great that he resorted to magnifying every interaction and glorifying his involvement.

He created a mental filter that was interfering with his effectiveness.

A colleague of mine pointed out the same observation, and we agreed that this leader's outcome would most likely be a derailed career if he continued along this path. People who project strength don't need the extra ego boost because their presence speaks for itself. And nobody likes a braggart.

OUR PRE-EXISTING CONDITIONS

We unlearn confidence over time.

I hate to throw out the *"you were probably traumatized as a child"* card, but psychology experts identify parental attitudes as a key factor in development. Parents who encourage kids to be self-reliant in a loving way pave a solid foundation of confidence. Conversely, a child's capacity to be secure about herself is damaged by parents who are excessively critical, demanding, and overprotective.

When parents facilitate a belief in kids that they are incapable, inadequate, or inferior, it leads to dependence on others for direction that carries into adulthood. I call this a *pre-existing condition*. These are exceptionally strong mental filters that take time to undo. People may not even realize these are in play, but once they bubble to the surface, they can be dealt with.

What life experiences have you had that that form your beliefs today?

Do you recognize some of your own pre-existing conditions? How have those conditions impacted the way you respond? Here are some examples:

- ° You feel guilty or ashamed when asking for help
- ° You get uncomfortable when things don't happen in order
- ° You stay quiet because you don't want to oppose authority

The mental filters you've applied are standing in your way of showing up with authentic executive presence.

Many of them are fear and guilt based, so it's important to identify those things and work through them. It's so critical, in fact, that you should take time to dig into what filters may exist for you currently, starting now.

GETTING "STUN-GUNNED"

Have you ever seen someone being zapped with a stun gun? People describe it as an intense electric shock that races through your body while it incapacitates your ability to move. The moment holds you captive; you forget to breathe until the jolt suddenly releases you and you crumple to the ground. You find yourself heaving like you just ran a 500-yard sprint and your muscles are worn out.

Now imagine that you are in a meeting as the center of attention, and you're moving along with fluid momentum with the point you are making. Without warning, you're abruptly cut off by a terse individual who sucks the air out of the room with some kind of unexpected emotional outburst. A cloud of heated smoke comes from his ears and he disputes your data or even attacks you as a person.

You are transformed into a stripped down peon, standing defenseless as your thoughts are debilitated. I call this getting *stun-gunned.*

Getting stun-gunned is the most feared experience of people who lead presentations or run meetings.

No amount of physical beauty or protective armor will prevent a stun-gun moment from happening. In fact, I would challenge that your chances of getting attacked are increased partly due to others' insecurities in the room. Hopefully, you won't ever go through that, but if you have, the effects can initially be shocking. Let's be clear; the people in the room may be able to temporarily maim your confidence, but you are not to blame for their behavior. You will recover in time.

You won't change those people, BUT you can change yourself and the way you react to them.

Allow that truth to sink deep into your heart and soul. It is worth remembering in times of trouble. There's always going to be a tug of war between having faith that things will work out and the fear that tries to knock you down.

Faith and fear are foes.

We all have certain skills, knowledge, or an area of expertise, but we tend to lose trust in our gifts when we put an unhealthy focus on the opinions of others, and live in fear of not meeting their standards. Which one will you let win?

A TRUE STUN GUN EXPERIENCE

I found myself in a perplexing scenario one morning as I presented a new departmental strategy to a group of my peers, all of them high-level leaders. My reporting team was there, sitting in anticipation, pumped up and sure that everyone would be in complete awe of the plan that we created. Being new to the company, I was delighted that we came together with a finalized plan in short amount of time. I was totally surprised at the turn of events that would shake my personal foundation.

The all-woman meeting came together in semi-cordial fashion with the customary *"How are you doing?"* introduction. As we settled in, the stage was set with two team members who would present the first segments. Both ladies were incredibility bright and spoke with enthusiasm. Each had spent hours structuring their presentations, bouncing them off our team to ensure everything was perfectly said and placed. This was a very proud moment for me as their leader, and I was pleased with their work. All was well so far.

My peers all sat at one table directly in front of the presenters. As I scouted for reactions from them, I noticed each one held a stoic expression. It seemed a bit comical, like the whole encounter was a spelling bee and they were there to judge, ready to ring the bell when a word was misspelled. I remained upbeat, however, knowing that my peers had a tendency to be a little uptight.

"It's probably a touch of boredom," I said to myself. I knew that my team had shared some high level information with everyone prior to the meeting as part of our communication plan.

It came time for me to deliver my portion of the presentation, and I expected the plan to generate positive affirmation. After all, I had been through this multiple times before with other organizations and succeeded. This encounter shouldn't be any different.

I began sharing the last half of the strategy, and felt a negative energy permeate the room as three of my peers began attacking like a swarm of bees. The atmosphere was confusing and hostile. Instead of curiosity, the questions were meant to sting and disable the strategy. I was blindsided and internally shocked, but externally resilient and calm.

The meeting finally came to an awkward close as people exited the room in a hurry. My team and I stayed behind. Up to this point I kept a game face, but when I saw their shocked and deflated faces, I broke down in tears and apologized to them that they had to go through the experience. We had been stun-gunned. It was a yucky moment for all of us. We were completely vulnerable and unaware of the surprise beehive party.

The experience was mortifying, but it taught me to always anticipate opposition, even in the best of circumstances.

I now teach others to explore possible blindsides and how to prepare for them.

Over time, two of the three came back and apologized, and the pain wore off. The damage to my personal confidence was temporary, and I came back to the truth of the matter, "You can't change anyone else, you can only change yourself and how you react to them." I also did a lot of personal reflection about how I handled that and incorporated a strategy for possible *stun guns* in the future.

If you have been through a stun-gun experience, it hurts and temporarily paralyzes you, but it doesn't kill you. I believe the majority of people who are confident risk takers will have this experience. When it happens, you have to work through it.

Your greatest move in overcoming the stun gun effect is forgiveness.

Holding others in a grudge sucks the life out of you like a cancer. YOU are the one who loses your presence, and YOU are the one who comes across as a bitter victim. While you may go through a grieving process, use the experience to reflect on what you would do differently in the next situation (while you drown your sorrows in a large bowl of macaroni and cheese or a hot fudge brownie sundae). Get comfortable with the idea that there will be a next time.

I believe that anyone who gets in front of leaders should learn to expect the stun gun to come out at any point.

It starts with NOT focusing on others, but operating from your authentic self and preparing ahead of time for potential *stun-gunning.*

From Self-Imprisoned to Self-Empowered

Bad experiences, grudges, and pre-existing conditions tend to hit your core confidence hard, and it's common to take on a victim mentality. While it might be okay for a minute, you can get stuck there, creating an invisible prison that prevents you from moving forward.

You could be disheartened or even brokenhearted, but staying in prison is your choice. Put on the Armor of Courage.

Courage is driven by your *bigger yes*. This means standing in the face of adversity, advocating for what you believe in and representing what is right—no matter what. You also need to find a spirit of resilience that repels the negativity and doubt that shoots its poisonous arrows at you. The good news is that you always live in choice, and you don't have to be chained to a life of self-depreciation. Let's use the plight of the circus elephant as an example of how we get stuck.

When a baby elephant is brought into the circus world, he's tied to a ground-anchored pole. His trainer disciplines him to become submissive, and the huge mammal learns not to strive. Over time, he becomes conditioned to accept his circumstances and withdraws at any sign of pain, and his fear has won.

The circus elephant matures into an adult, graduating from his baby weight of 300 pounds to an astronomical mass of up to 12,000 pounds. Unaware of his potentially devastating power over the anchored pole, he is a prisoner capable of escaping, but has no concept of his ability to do so.

You have the power to free yourself from the prison of damaged confidence.

It starts with identifying the victimizing beliefs you are anchored to and are holding close to your heart. Did somebody tell you that you suck? Were you minimized in front of a crowd? Whatever the reason, it's important to recognize and separate yourself from those beliefs. You can start pulling against the pole with a simple realization:

Whatever comes out of a person's mouth is a direct indication of what lives inside.

In other words, people behave like idiots sometimes because they have their own scruples, and they are taking it out on others. That has nothing to do with you. Maybe you *did* deserve some kind of feedback, but the person didn't deliver it with a ton of emotional intelligence. Recognize the situation for what it is and quit wallowing in sorrow. You don't have to own anyone's emotional challenges.

Yank that anchored pole out of the ground and walk away from the circus.

I encourage you to be meticulous about empower-ing yourself from the inside out, as opposed to outside in. Remember this is a two-part journey that includes the management of impressions, and investing in the evaluation-based characteristics that lead to long-term success. I chuckle when I see internet self-help articles that give superficial advice like *love yourself* and *dress better.* *"Gosh, why didn't I think of that before? And I will be sure to love myself and wear the suggested outfit! Thanks, Mr. Internet Advisor!"*

Seriously, take time to be introspective. If you want to do a deep dive on how to build confidence, I encourage you to explore *The School of Executive Presence™* at *www.schoolofexecutivepresence.com,* which will help you develop deep self-awareness around your strengths and sensitivities, as well as test your courage levels.

CHAPTER 3

PIES: The Pieces of Success

SPOTLIGHT: FROM UNKNOWN TO UNFORGETTABLE

If you boil it down, it was a social business experiment. 30 people in a corporate setting were invited to participate in a unique talent discovery program for one year, many of them unknown to the senior leadership of a Fortune 500 company.

The participants were a diverse group from all parts of the organization. All of them were performing well, but not well known by leaders. Through a series of development experiences, coaching, genuine project work, and purposeful visibility events, they were able to break through to the executive level.

The program went beyond promotional opportunities, and it was a life changer for many people. Some worked through mental filters and personal obstacles that freed them up to be authentic and more valuable to the company—and their leaders were in awe. Some participants even reported that life at home had changed for the better because of their growth at work.

Winning hearts and minds of hiring managers was a great side effect of the program. Participants were getting high visibility with decision makers looking for their next team superstar, while also digging into meaningful work that was formally recognized. At the end of the year, at least 30% had taken on a new role, and several more have contacted me since then who have advanced their careers.

Tony Rondinella, a program alumni, recalls his experience at the time:

"I was completely focused on my performance and had the mindset that, as long as I did great work, career advancement would take care of itself. I quickly realized the existence and importance of my image and exposure. I began focusing on enhancing my strengths instead of trying so hard to close the gap on my opportunities. I discovered I had talents and skills that could transcend business roles. I would never have been aware of or considered these had it not been for my expanded focus that went beyond my performance.

For the first time in my career, I'm being purposeful about targeting my next role in a completely unfamiliar business unit due to recognition of the alignment of my passions and strengths with the work of the organization. I've successfully established a network and have found opportunities to build my image through working on side projects."

Yesterday, Tony was unknown. Today, he is moving toward his purpose and calling. Tomorrow, he will be unforgettable when it's time for his next mission.

CONVERTING CREDIBILITY TO CAREER AND ORGANIZATIONAL SUCCESS

Executive presence is built upon credibility, but the challenge is converting it to *career and organizational success* in business. After all, isn't that a major motivating factor in the quest to maximize our presence? Who doesn't want to be successful? It doesn't necessarily mean that you want to become the CEO of the company (although it may); you might be looking to be known for your expertise in a certain area or want to be recognized for what you contribute to your company mission.

Regardless of your career goal, you need a formula working in your life.

Success is perpetuated by an interesting concept I call PIES, and there are four pieces:

° *Performance*
° *Image*
° *Exposure*
° *Social agility*

Harvey Coleman, author of *Empowering Yourself: The Organizational Game Revealed,* introduced the first three pieces many years ago after studying the unwritten rules of organizational influence, politics, and promotions. Coleman asserts in his book that performance, image, and exposure have a certain percentage value in your career equation.

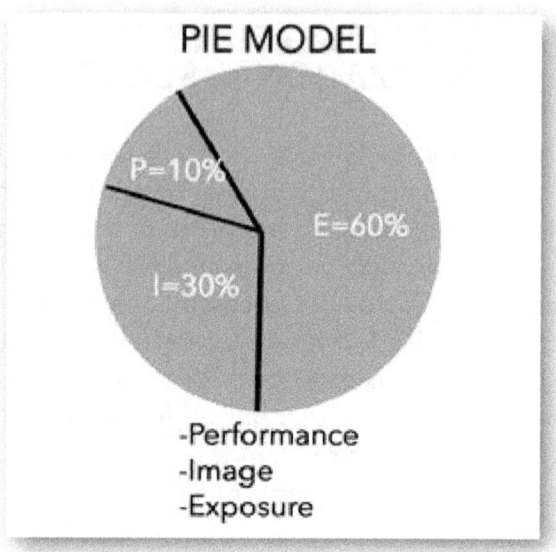

Those percentages may be shocking, but the story at the beginning of the chapter was based on this model, and I am here to tell you that it is a real phenomenon.

I see the first three pieces of PIE being described like this:

- **Performance:** Your actual work output, your technical skills and abilities, as well as the quality results you get from your work
- **Image:** How you show up from a personal branding standpoint to others, your self-awareness, credibility, doing what you say you will do (DWYSYWD)
- **Exposure:** Your networking prowess, building and maintaining relationships

PIE is alive and well in the business world. However, there's one missing piece we need to add in order to articulate what's really happening in meetings, boardrooms, and daily interactions. Our PIE becomes plural: PIES.

SOCIAL AGILITY AND PIES

I'm sure you've heard, "It's not what you know, but who you know." Well, there may be some truth to that statement, but I propose that you need some social agility in the mix to really be successful.

You can be a great performer, have all the self-awareness in the world with a big network, but if you aren't able to read the environment, be intuitive about the people around you and their needs, you will struggle.

The addition of social agility as a PIE piece alters the percentages that Coleman identifies in his model. Based on my experience as a talent and organizational development practitioner, the percentage balance looks like this:

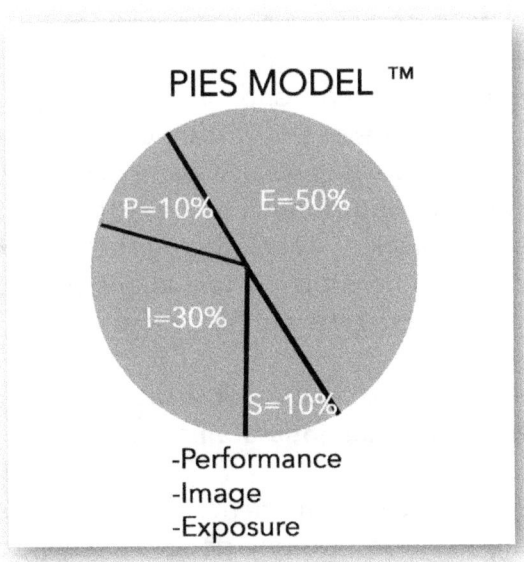

PIES MODEL ™

P=10% E=50%
I=30%
S=10%

-Performance
-Image
-Exposure

I often ask people to guess what piece of PIES is most important in terms of percentage breakdown before I show them the graph.

90% believe performance is the most influential factor and exposure is the least. This is not the case.

While performance equates to only 10%, it's a very critical 10% that has to be stellar.

Performance is only the entry ticket.

Social agility is also a very important 10% that gives an edge to your success, and the research leans heavily upon the social element as a factor. As you can see, performance and image is about you, while exposure and social agility focuses outward to others. You simply can't get away with obliviousness toward your surroundings when you are trying to achieve successful business outcomes.

I equate the percentage breakdowns in terms of *energy output*, *time investment*, and *order*. Your performance should already be present. If you are operating within your strengths and natural talents, it's just a matter of tweaking and honing what you do well to perfect it. On the personal side, your work on image through self-awareness and internal focus is a nonstop job that keeps you honest with yourself and others. Here's a vital tidbit:

Performance and image are realized only if you have an audience AND you understand their needs.

If you have great performance and you have a handle on yourself, it doesn't do any good if others don't know

you exist. If people know you're there, but you aren't pay-
ing attention to their needs, they will lose interest in you
fast.

Again, don't underestimate the power of any of these
pieces. Social agility adds 10%, but if you omit this important ingredient, it's the equivalent of leaving out the sugar
or the teaspoon of baking powder in a recipe.

PIES EXAMPLE: AMERICAN IDOL

American Idol, in its early years, is a good example of how
PIES manifests in organizations. If you've ever watched this
popular reality show, you know that thousands of entertainers audition every year in hopes of becoming the next
singing superstar. The people who prove their natural talent with exceptional vocal technique get to move on to the
Hollywood Week round.

Reminder: Performance is only the entry ticket.

Occasionally, people who don't have the best vocals
get a ticket to Hollywood Week. These novel entertainers
don't last long in the grueling process because the judges
demand exceptional and consistent performance. People
start to unravel emotionally and abandon self-awareness as
they struggle to fit in.

*Image shows up externally in the form of emotional
intelligence and maturity.*

The field is narrowed significantly as the top 24 move along
the journey. These are the competitors with genuine talent.

Most people who get into Hollywood Week through dramatic shock value or cuteness have been eliminated because the novelty has worn off and there's no substance left. The exposure piece is now seeping in as the 12 guys and 12 gals are thrust into a televised spotlight for public scrutiny over the next several weeks.

Now the real competition begins. Each week, a sensational popularity contest ensues and singers are methodically eliminated through public vote. There's usually some type of controversy over who gets kicked off the show, and it's always someone with brilliant vocals. Why does this happen? I assert it's because that person hasn't connected with the audience as well as other contestants. A relationship has to be built, not only with the judges, but also with the viewers.

Stakes are high as the remaining contestants are reduced to single digits in the final weeks. The time has come when exposure and social smarts must now be evoked as each person thinks through a strategy that appeals to the masses. Emotions must be reached, souls need to be stirred, and a song that fuses these elements with the singer's authentic being has to be propagated to get to the final round.

Two finalists are left standing, and the public has chosen sides. These two performers have shown up masterfully week after week. Who will be the victor? It will be the person who has maximized all pieces of PIES, but has truly activated the social agility aspect more than his or her competitor. Unanimous favor may not have been won, but the new American Idol has edged out the runner up by striking a relational cord in the most positive way with the audience. That person has learned how to incorporate the right ingredients and slice their PIES appropriately.

EXAMINING YOUR OWN PIES

You need all the pieces of PIES. Let's take a look at some general questions you should be asking yourself in each piece:

P-Performance:
- Am I doing my best work?
- Is my work high quality or high quantity?
- Do my performance reviews at work reflect how well I am really doing in my job?

I-Image:
- What am I known for?
- What feedback do I get from others about my personality?
- What actions have I taken to become a better person emotionally, spiritually, and physically?
- What personal attributes are standing in the way of my success?

E-Exposure:
- How often do I step outside my office or cubicle to talk to people?
- How many new relationships am I building each month?
- What percentage of the organization knows who I am?
- How well would I say my community knows me?

S-Social Agility:
- When I walk into a meeting, what is the first thing I typically do?

°   What percentage of the time am I talking in meet-
    ings? Listening?
°   How do I know when to speak, when to act, and
    when to do neither?

So, some words of advice: Remember that you need
to balance your PIES, so distribute your efforts accord-
ingly. In other words, you don't want to spend 80% of your
time working on performance (unless it's *grossly* deficient).
Ensure that you are building your network and relationships as you go along, as well as working on your image
and brand. Social agility will be a big focus as you grow,
and becoming more aware of your environment will be a
gradual process.

I want to mention this important factor. We have a tendency to become the *emperor with no clothes*. It's easy
to recognize how others are showing up with total lack
of self-awareness, but we are all in the same boat. What
blind spots are there for you? How can you know what they
are? Avoid the temptation to go it alone and risk avoidable
humiliation. Invite a friend or colleague to give you feedback along the way. You will be glad you did.

CHAPTER 4

A Deep Dive on Social Agility

SPOTLIGHT: THE KING OF SOCIAL AGILITY

Scott Pothoven is a business director in a food ingredient production and manufacturing environment with global responsibility. His knack for being socially agile is incredible. Here's his story.

" I want to solve world peace AND world hunger!" Scott is a well-dressed, clean-cut man with a big heart. He also holds a big responsibility assisting with operations in Nepal and Africa. Back home in the good ole USA, he's heading up a new leadership development program to get leaders positioned for a new vision and mission for the company. He knows the business well and lives its mission.

Executives in his organization point out, "People just flock to him when he comes in the door. He's like a magnet; everyone knows him and loves him."

It's magical to witness Scott observing the room during a leadership workshop. He searches each face, reading reactions and anticipating concerns. He can spot trouble a mile away and will meet it with a smile and enthusiasm. His body language is open and he is easily approachable. His words are powerful and inspiring, and leaders receive him as kind, inviting, yet tenacious.

"I just want everyone to feel like they are loved and appreciated. And I want them to know Jesus."

Scott definitely has a gift of intuition, and it's even more apparent in times of challenge. With multiple changes happening with the culture, people need comfort. Scott is there, heading up employee forums, dealing with angst, and ensuring transparent two-way communication between employees, leaders, and executives.

He's definitely the King of Social Agility. And he's probably going to at least help his company solve world hunger.

FROM THE INSIDE OUT

True executive presence begins on the inside and works its way out. We open the door to the rest of society and we're met with perceptions, preferences, and judgments. Figuring out a way to manage these forces takes quite a bit of skill.

It's a tough world and we will never please everyone. When we try to jump the hoops the world gives us, we begin to lose ourselves, our authenticity diminishes, and confidence erodes. There has to be a happy medium. We have to understand what blaring obstacles are in our way of connecting with people. It's not appropriate to completely dismiss them, so what do we do?

Let's think about it from an executive chef's perspective.

HOW AN EXECUTIVE CHEF WORKS

Most high-end chefs are respected and sought out for their ability to bring the right ingredients, portions, and artistry to the table. They know when they are serving baby milk-fed lamb, a top quality Bordeaux, burgundy, or Rioja mature wine is the best pairing. If the entrée is a pink centered spring lamb with fresh herbs, a Pinot Noir or cru Beaujolais would be a better fit.

The executive chef has all the skills and ingredients necessary for a splendid evening, but skillful planning and observance is the key to a delightful experience.

Quality chefs preparing for a private party will explore who the guests will be and their preferences. He directs the questions to learn what options to present, but he is also looking for what is unsaid. Reactions, body language, word choice—everything is compiled mentally to be sorted out and distilled down to what will excite the taste buds of the guests. Still, Chef has the advantage because he can influence the food choices and ultimately decides what will be served. After all, this is his area of expertise, and the delivery will be flawless.

The timing in which each meal course is delivered is critical. A true executive chef has his kitchen in order, meticulously managing it like a musical orchestra. He calls the kitchen to bring forth dessert to the stage, a decadent chocolate soufflé with poached pear, touched with salted caramel. Chef knows the soufflé is added immediately before it goes out, otherwise the pears will sweat.

Equally important is the traditional "check-in", where Chef ensures the patrons are enjoying their meal while purposely driving them to connect the fabulous food with his name and brand.

He is a people manager and influencer, so he gets a read on how the experience is going, doing damage control in case some small detail has been overlooked.

Occasionally, a rogue patron misbehaves. The confident Chef knows this patron's outburst is easily a play for attention, so he listens calmly and respectfully. He assesses the people around this disruptive soul, and gathers intelligence before he acts. Is this person alone in his belief, or are others on board with his outburst?

He looks to resolve the issue without ever owning the patron's emotions and personal baggage, bringing about a clever response that will neutralize skewed attitudes.

He begins to speak in a way that heightens his credibility with the guests, softening their weakened blows until they have to give in to his realness. He offers a solution, and they gratefully accept.

YOU'RE THE CHEF IN THE ROOM

This is your role. You have all the ingredients you need, and you probably have a "preferred menu" of skills you like to use. You are authentic, gifted, and you have reason to be confident. Your audience may have different personalities and hang-ups, but you aren't responsible for their behavior and you at least want to remain consistent in your approach. Your job is to explore, plan, and leverage your people intelligence to increase the likelihood of a positive reaction.

Ultimately, you are looking for agreement, not approval.

This is important to digest as you learn more about the topic of social agility.

SOCIAL AGILITY: IT SOUNDS COOL, BUT WHAT DOES IT MEAN?

Social agility requires flexibility to create a relationship between you and your audience. You can use it to think through your interactions with people before, during, and after you are with them.

I define social agility in this way:

Assessing, perceiving, and flexing your behavior so your audience will hear you and come to an agreement with you, while consistently maintaining your authenticity and confidence.

It isn't just about you, my friend.

It's also about being fully present with the people around you and having positive engagement with them. You are looking for a mutual win where both parties will benefit. This means showcasing your attributes that best represent your goal, while pulling back the things that could distract people from buying in. When you do this, you are practicing good social agility.

People react well to you and are even drawn to you because you see, hear, and understand them. You then give them what they really need.

THE ELEMENTS OF SOCIAL AGILITY

Karl Albrecht, author of *Social Intelligence: The New Science of Success,* calls out terms like *social smarts* and *situational awareness* as important to one's overall success with other people. I agree wholeheartedly that you have to read the room and understand what makes people tick, but social agility goes beyond a meeting.

You have to consider your culture and overall business environment.

You also have to manage certain aspects of yourself to gain agreement with people, and this requires adaptation. Let's look at a few important elements of social agility and gain a high level view of how it works.

1. Assess The Environment.

The first step of walking into a business meeting is to open your eyes, ears, and mouth. You start with the obvious signs of how people are feeling, what they are saying, and what they are doing.

- ° What are their facial expressions?
- ° How are people positioned? Where are they sitting? Are they standing?
- ° Is there a central figure in the room? How are others responding to him/her?
- ° Are they quiet, talking to others, or having intimate side conversations?
- ° What is the mood? Tense? Relaxed? Cordial?
- ° What are people doing with their hands? Writing? Motioning? Showing white knuckles?
- ° What nonverbal communication are you observing?
- ° Do their words, actions, and facial expressions align?

As you listen and observe, you should be moving about the room greeting people, shaking hands, and checking in to see what's on their minds.

Human touch is extremely powerful, not only in establishing a relationship, but also in reading a person's status.

- ° What kind of handshake are you experiencing from the other person? Tight grip? Assertive? Wimpy?
- ° Do they look you in the eye or do their eyes drop to the floor?
- ° What vibe do you get when you are talking? Are they troubled? Happy?
- ° Are they showing interest in what you have to say, or are they inattentive?
- ° How are people responding to your presence in the room? Are you the center of attention? Acknowledged by a few folks? Invisible?

You may be overwhelmed and thinking, *Oh my Lord! How could I ever track all this stuff in just a few minutes?* I promise it's very possible. I've coached people and conducted workshops around this complex but achievable skill. Even the most structure-minded engineers learn to develop it over time.

Smart people think through a plan before they ever enter a meeting, playing through possible scenarios and determining how they will handle it.

Your environmental assessment helps you formulate some general conclusions so you can act according to your plan. For example, if the initial room conversation is cordial and light, you know that immediately starting a conversation about an impending layoff or the recent product scandal might not be a good idea. Prepare to talk about the tough topics, but use your planning and assessment to determine the best timing.

2. Perceive and gain organizational savvy.

Individuals who want to effectively contribute to the company mission research ways to understand the relevant business activities. They connect to multiple people and information sources to find out how the company is doing financially, who is operating in what role, what the latest products are, and how the business challenges are being met.

Knowing every detail is not required, but learning enough to be dangerous is helpful.

This is the perceiving part. What details are important? What would be considered *enough to be dangerous*? Ultimately, the person who practices organizational savvy is able to adapt to the environment and become a prominent player.

You'll have an advantage if you understand clearly how your role fits into the overall picture. The business mission should be driving all activities, and it's important for you to learn how departments or business functions connect to it—and to you. You can accomplish fast learning if you incorporate this goal into your PIES *exposure* plan.

As you meet people, ask them to teach you about their roles and how they support the business.

Dig deeper into the personal aspects, like what's important to them in the daily job, or how they perceive certain dynamics in the organization.

Spend time each week researching outside of your organization.

Who are your competitors? What do they possess? What is the outside perception of your company? How do you stack up financially? Equally important is the cultural perception of your employer. Sites like LinkedIn, Glass Door, and Salary.com give unfiltered feedback and information that can be folded into your analysis.

As you take in what you are given and draw perceptions, find ways to apply them to your work.

Fold them into your conversations with others. Ask questions about what they think or ideas they have. Add newly learned insights to your presentations and meeting updates. Suggest and implement solutions that help the company be more effective. To be organizationally savvy, you have to step out of any silos that currently exist in your world, start talking the company language in a way that fits your values, and show up in a way that demonstrates your genuine care of business success.

3. Flex and adapt to the cultural blueprint.

You've got to be a part of the company culture in order to be genuinely effective. I'm talking about living and talking the mission, vision, and values that typically instigate all business activities.

When you bring a large body of people together, a social norms blueprint develops with an expectation of adherence.

Your willingness to adapt without compromising your personal values is crucial.

Reflect upon this willingness. Executive presence is not about selling yourself out and becoming someone you are not. It's about respecting the values of your organization and accepting the situation for what it is while trying to facilitate improvement. You can still thrive and even be a change agent while maintaining the relationship.

We tend to get stymied at this point because we aren't thinking in terms of win-win. Our belief that we are right and someone is wrong creates a huge obstacle in our path to success.

A person with authentic presence doesn't get hung up on this, but rather learns to appreciate the diversity of thought through curiosity and solution-focused questions.

Yes, there are creepy people out there who lack a moral compass, but I've witnessed them strategically disarmed through respectful challenge.

Ponder these questions.

° Where do you really fit into the culture, and where do you want to fit?
° Do your values align with those of your organization?
° If you are experiencing a cultural conflict, is it more toward a specific person, a group of people, or the organization as a whole?

If you aren't in agreement with a person or group of people, you can usually work through the pain. *If you are working for a company that provides services or products you don't believe in, you probably need to be looking for employment elsewhere.*

4. More Flexing: Style.

Style is an extension of your image. Your brain has a default process for taking in data and coming to decisions a certain way. You may have taken one or more of the popular personality assessments like Myers Briggs Type Indicator, DISC, or StrengthsFinder, which help with style awareness.

The important thing to remember is that you can maximize your style and play to your natural strengths.

You can also minimize those pieces of your personality that can be distracting or annoying to others. Talking about this subject in depth would require me to write another book altogether, so I want to draw your attention to five specific influencers that can help or hurt your executive presence:

- ° Your *look*
- ° How you *show up*
- ° How you *think*
- ° The *words* you *speak*
- ° The sound of your *voice*

These are the parts of you that surface when you interact with the business. All of those wonderful attributes you hold inside are not immediately visible to your audience.

You have to knock down as many initial barriers as you can so they can see the real you.

All five fit into three general categories.

If you've ever gone through any kind of presentation or facilitation training, you've probably heard of the *3 Vs (visual, vocal, and verbal)*. I teach people that we all go through a brain related process when someone presents to us.

There's an order in which we take in data.

1. **Visually:** Our brain is naturally drawn to what the person is wearing, how he or she looks, facial

expressions, gestures, eye contact, and general movement. I call this a *survival and trust mechanism.* We don't hear much until we interpret what we're experiencing, and then we come to some type of conclusion about what we are seeing. Some experts say that over half of your initial credibility is decided by your look.

2. ***Vocally:*** We now focus on how the person is speaking. We listen for volume, inflection, pausing, pace, and diction. The sound of a voice can intrigue us, or it can lull us to sleep. The way our words flow together is also a factor in keeping the attention of the audience. We ask ourselves, *Is this person interesting and inviting?* We don't like boring speakers, and our brains move on to other thoughts if our interest isn't peaked.

3. ***Verbally:*** I don't want to imply that words are least important of the three, but they're last to be recognized by our brains. I assure you that verbiage and its structure are critical, but we have to get through the barriers of visual and vocal cues to hear what's being said.

    Our brain listens for recognizable words and gets confused by long, extraneous pontifications (like the last two words). If we repeat words, we pick up their patterns of use. Have you ever had someone overuse a word or phrase to the point that you are distracted by it and can't hear the rest of the message? It happens often. You may be aware of this, but you probably have words that you could manage or eliminate from your own dictionary.

Style can be a big deal breaker in terms of earning credibility in your organization, so it's important to find out how others are experiencing you.

Hopefully you've already sought feedback in this area and know what's working, and what isn't. If you want to learn more about your style, visit *The School of Executive Presence* at www.schoolofexecutivepresence.com to take an assessment so you can gain awareness on how you may be impacting others. The site also offers a 360 option to solicit feedback from the people around you.

CHAPTER 5

Insights, Tips, and Tools

LET'S GET PRACTICAL!

I'd like to help you become more self-aware through practical recommendations and tools around the 5 Influencers. You may have some preconceived notions or beliefs around each one, and I want to offer some insights based on my experience in dealing with the business world. I also want to offer some tips and tools that can really make your desire for a successful career attainable.

1. Your "Look".

The topic of a person's look is almost always controversial, particularly in the corporate world. Research shows it's important, but it's not the long term determining factor to your success. In reality, people make initial decisions based on what you look like and what you wear. Traditionalists believe that the unisex black conservative suit is most appropriate. As the world culture is changing, we see rebel executives coming out of the woodwork wearing jeans and tee-shirts to their board meetings. Others might sport a new tattoo or a nose piercing. What is considered appropriate, and who is right?

There are three factors to consider:

° **Culture:** What seems to be the norm regarding appearance and attire?
° **Your Personal Style**: What is genuinely important to you about the way you appear or dress—so much so that you need to make a statement about it?
° **The Setting:** Is this a high stakes meeting where you are trying to gain buy-in? Who is attending and what's important to them?

Get distracting things out of the way while allowing your unique style to draw people in.

Wearing your bell bottoms and tie dye shirt to the executive level meeting with a room full of traditionalists won't win you many points, so pick and choose your battles wisely. You can still shine with your personal style while incorporating aspects of the culture and setting.

Ask yourself these questions:

° What message do I want to send in the way I dress or appear?

- ° Will my look detract from my message, and which is more important to me?
- ° What can I do to demonstrate my personal style without becoming a clone of the environment?

Let's say you love brightly colored clothing that shows your artistic side. You know the group you'll be interacting with is conservative. You don't want people to miss your message because they're so mesmerized by your multicolored top with shiny things. How do you compromise so that it's classy? Wear the artistic top with a conservative jacket, which sends a subliminal message: *"I respect the cultural norms, and I also have a unique perspective that keeps things interesting."* This aligns with the win-win mindset, an important way to be thinking where dress is concerned.

People appreciate someone who dresses neat and clean with flair of style.

When the audience first meets you, they will be checking out your appearance first as part of the mental checklist. Don't be crossed off the list because your style overpowers the room. Conversely, don't get overlooked because you have an underwhelming presence or show up as an exact replica of everyone else.

Small doses work.

Occasionally, I see executives looking away to avoid being distracted by the person's appearance. This happened to me in an executive presentation with the corporate CEO. As I was sharing, he stared at the table and refused to look up at me. I was initially offended by this, but realized he was simply trying to hear the message. He eventually looked up as we began the open forum of discussion with the rest of the executives, and I breathed a sigh of relief.

Visual "listeners" sometimes get distracted by objects or colors, so they zone out for a minute and miss the message.

Now, if you see someone looking down because they are reading their text messages, that is a different story and you may need to step up your wow factor.

Here are some additional tips to ensure you are getting your message across without distractions:

1. **Be mindful of the basics.** Wear clean and wrinkle free clothing that truly gives you a sense of pride and confidence. This includes clean shoes free from scuffs. For ladies, I recommend avoiding the 5-inch spiky hooker pumps and platform shoes, they tend to lessen your credibility and they are uncomfortable to walk in. Also, beware of your behind. Honestly, people do look at your backside so be mindful that tight pants show your underwear lines and make camel toes in the front. It's funny but frightful when it happens, and it does. Nobody wants to be the "butt" of a joke by earning nick-names like *Carla Camel Toe* or *Patty Panty Lines*.

2. **Wear clothes you feel powerful in.** You probably have everyday clothes that are comfortable, but I encourage you to experiment with different colors

and styles that give you a sense of energy and confidence. Get someone to give you feedback so you don't default to your favorite 20-year-old frumpy sweater and black polyester pants. If you dig the traditional corporate suit, good for you, but add some color that shows you can think for yourself. I challenge you to experiment in order to discover what clicks. You would be amazed at how fashion instigates conversations, particularly for women. "That's a beautiful shirt, where did you get it?"

3. *Share your flair.* For guys, ties are a great way to showcase your style. Ties serve as a conversation piece and make you more approachable. For ladies, accent jewelry has the same effect and has become a symbol of personality. Use this to express yourself. Remember the golden rule of giving your style in small doses, however, to avoid overwhelming people with chaotic or blatant body visuals.

4. *Don't be a clown; keep make-up toned down.* Overdoing the shimmery blue eye shadow, painted on eyebrows, and bright red lipstick sends the message that you are insecure and have to hide your face. You are going for classy, not trashy. For guys, be careful about using black hair dye and hairpieces. Some people interpret that in the same way as a woman with heavy make-up—fake and insecure.

5. *Be informative about piercings, tattoos, or other expressive visuals.* There's a shift happening regarding these forms of expressions and they have become sociably acceptable. However, most traditionalists don't understand them and still hold biases. I recommend that if you have prominent tattoo art or metal that's visible to others, call it out

as part of your discussion so people can move on from their fixation and hear your message. If you plan to display piercings, be prepared to share why it's important to you if you are working in a conservative environment.

Keep in mind there are many beliefs and perceptions about the way you look. One belief is that you have to have physical beauty to capture attention. Not true. Good looks are a temporary attention grabber, but then people move on to other evaluations of you. You can learn more by conducting your own social experiment or even polling people about their thoughts on the subject.

2. The Way You Show Up.

The way you show up is visually processed and filed into mental notes. You get credibility points when you demonstrate consistency and alignment between your actions and your words. You *lose* points when you overstate or understate your personality.

It's like being on a reality TV show. You develop storylines with your behavior.

People apply perceptions to the situation, and then draw conclusions about you. Some people create drama to get more attention, but the novelty is temporary and those people fade out (or get kicked off the show). We're usually pulling for the one who shows up with authenticity, respect, and emotional intelligence. We want them to overcome the situation and succeed, and in the process they win our hearts.

Getting to this place requires you to be at peace with yourself, be proactive with transparency, and operate with integrity. Don't think this means that you have to be perfect. We relate to others who aren't perfect if they are honest and working on it.

Your body language can draw or erase credibility.

Your audience catalogues the way you move your hands, head, and body. They want to see if your movements are consistent with your words. They can also sense when you're feeling uncomfortable. It's easy to recognize a nervous, inexperienced presenter when you see him or her doing what I call the *penguin fin whirly bird:* Shoulders are scrunched, elbows are pinned close to the body, and hands are creating an awkward propeller type motion.

Be mindful of your use of hands; they should flow with the presentation. Other things to manage include:

- ° Facial Expressions
- ° Movement (too much pacing or no movement at all hurts your presence)
- ° Sitting during a presentation (don't do it)
- ° Posture (stay away from the hunchback)
- ° Rocking back and forth (you'll make people sea sick)

Remember that you don't have the license to be a jerk.

You have vulnerabilities and imperfections, and it's not an excuse to be indifferent or resigned to being stuck there. I learned this lesson myself.

As a leader in the corporate world, I took my teams on "crazy idea" roller coaster rides at times. My thought was *Look people, this is how I'm built and you better jump in and strap your seatbelt on because we're going for a ride!* I would think of a vision and put it into motion immediately with fast results, and the organization loved it. My gift was also my curse. People would be frustrated, telling me to slow down, and I was giving the impression that I didn't listen.

One day, a good friend and colleague helped me realize I was using my great results as a reason not to change my approach.

"Bring people along with you and meet them where they're at."

Her feedback resonated with me and I adjusted my approach to one that included a lot more curious questions, idea generation, and feedback. I had to realize that not everybody thinks like me, and that's okay. I really worked hard at being more patient and open. Slowing down a bit actually helped me to get to a more peaceful place in my life—and the people around me appreciated it too.

Here are some other thoughts and tips about the impact of behavior:

1. ***You don't have to be an intellectual genius to be a bright bulb in the room.*** Many times we hurt our believability because we behave as if we know more than we really do. This tactic backfires in a hurry and people are quick to see through it. You are better off admitting you don't know but would like to learn more. You can also ask questions,

learn the necessary data, and strategically integrate it into your business activities and language. You will be respected for being real, and you will shine brighter in the room as a result.

2. ***Humor breaks down the barriers between you and your audience.*** You have a great gift if you have a knack for saying quirky things or popping out a spontaneous joke. Laughing makes people vulnerable to letting go of their composure a bit. If humor is a natural part of your personality make up, give them just enough to make them want more, as opposed to a whole buffet. I just recommend not overusing it. When you overdo it, people don't take you seriously and you lose more credibility points.

3. ***Take stock of your nonverbal behavior.*** People see what you are saying by what you aren't saying. You already know your facial expressions, your posture, and the position of your extremities all tell a tale. How do people know you are onboard with a decision, or unhappy about the business plan in the meeting? When you are disappointed, how does it manifest in your body? Do a social agility assessment on yourself. Seek feedback from a trusted friend or co-worker about how your nonverbals show up.

4. ***Respect the absent.*** Talking about other people when they aren't around is a big fat no-no. I've heard people try to circumvent this by saying, "Well, if Bob were here, I would say it to his face," or "I can share this because I've already given Linda that feedback." People hear you talking about others, and they assume you will be chatting about them when they aren't around. Again, you become

a bright bulb in the room when you abstain from talking about others and their imperfections.

5. ***Don't be the "Troll of Control".*** If you want to make people in the room uncomfortable, start trying to control everything or panic about your lack of control. I see great people who have a more structured and sequential mind short-circuit when things get out of order. They become uneasy when you show your discomfort, and it turns into some kind of crisis, "talk you off the ledge" experience where everyone is embarrassed afterward. The fact is that executive level meetings and presentations require adaptability to whatever comes next. Sometimes it can go from a calm sea of unity to a rapid-fire stun gun showdown. You need to accept that this can and will happen, so get comfortable with not knowing what to expect.

6. ***Tension brings opportunity.*** I find it fascinating how we say that conflict is needed, but when it shows up we freak out a bit. The next time this happens, watch the nonverbal behavior in the room tighten up with wide eyes, bunched up shoulders, and people fidgeting in their chairs. This is your chance to stand out, so start by not looking like the rest of the room. Take nice, deep, cleansing breaths, pull back your shoulders, smile, and relax. When you have the opportunity to speak or comment, be the light bulb in the room by doing the following:

   ° Acknowledge the tension so everyone can breathe ("I see there is excitement about this topic...")

- ° Ask powerful and curious questions to navigate through the political landmines ("What's really important about this topic to you?" "What would it look like if we_____?")
- ° If you disagree, have the courage to state your position respectfully and politely while giving a reason ("I have a different view about the project because our customer rated us low on service satisfaction.")

7. **Graduate from the high school clique mentality.** This isn't high school anymore where you have to be a replica of the football captain or prom queen. You've grown up and are a mature person with aspirations of solving world peace (or another meaningful goal). If you feel like you don't belong with the people in the room, take advantage of it and let your presence capture their attention. This is an opportunity to benefit from the uniqueness you bring, and you don't have to look like everyone else.

   We admire people who don't do group think, but have the guts to be creative with ideas while still engaging people in a positive way. At the end of the day, you have to be true to your values, who you are, and what you stand for. Standing by these things will be the most important factor.

   What I advise against is coming from an obnoxious place. I've seen so many people try to stand out by being the oppositional child in the room for the sake of argument. That will get you notoriety, not fame.

3. The Way You Think.

Have you ever been in the room when someone was speaking so eloquently that every thought melted together like butter on toast? The structure and meaning flowed flawlessly, and their message was crystal clear. Did you even wish you knew their secret?

Go to a different scenario where the person speaking appeared legitimate, but opened his or her mouth, and the trust in competence and credibility came crashing down. The words were so incredibly conceptual and unorganized that you were left to deal with the aftermath of a common question: "What in the world did that person just say?" You may have felt stupid afterwards.

I like how the Myers Briggs Type Indicator Assessment, a popular brain-related personality assessment, sheds light on our thinking structure. Our brain has a preference in how it likes to take in information, process data, make decisions, and then express a thought.

Some of us see the world concretely through the five senses, and some of us see it conceptually through pictures, patterns, and abstractness. As we process and decide what *it* is, we can now express *it*. There are those who have a very structured and sequential output of expression. Others have a free flowing, random, and spontaneous way of expressing thoughts. There's nothing wrong with either style, it's just that one may be better suited in one situation and less effective another situation.

I'll show you what I mean through a quick experiment. You will need a piece of paper and a timer. Allow yourself one minute to look at the picture (Figure A). After a minute, put the picture down and write down what you saw then go to the next page.

There are two general types of responses that occur in this exercise: "structured" and "big picture".

1. *The structured thinker does these things FIRST.*
   ° Likes to count items in the picture, like number of people
   ° Identifies objects, like a mirror
   ° Notices concrete things, like a group of people standing, person looking in the mirror
   ° Identifies colors

2. *The big picture thinker does these things FIRST.*
   ° Creates a story, like "a woman is not seeing who she really is and her colleagues are in the back making fun of her"
   ° Identifies things conceptually, like "her clothes stink and are dingy"
   ° May identify people and things, but only after the story has been created

Figure A

You may identify with both lists, but what did you see first? Did you start counting, or did you start storytelling? As you see, you've taken in information, processed it, and have come to a decision about it, which drives how you express yourself. Big picture thinkers speak conceptually, while structured thinkers tend to express themselves in a concrete and more orderly and sequential manner.

When you're speaking in a meeting or presentation, you need a mix of both styles.

Tell the story, and do it in a structured fashion. You can learn to balance your thoughts in a way that's clear, yet highly inspiring. You will just want to commit to learning some simple formulas. Here are two examples for you:

1. *Make Your Point Model.* I first heard this model being used by a wonderful lady I worked with, Jennifer Zinn. Use this model to clearly state your position on a particular matter when you are asked what you think about something. It is great for face-to face responses, as well as in emails.

   ° My position on_____
     is_____
   ° My reason is_____
   ° An example is_____
   ° And that's why my position is_____

   So here is an example of what it might sound like:
   *"My **position** on Yolanda being accepted into the program is that she should be able to*

participate. My **reason** is because she got a 4.3 on her performance review, and she is respected for her leadership style. To give you an **example**, she was selected by her peers and direct reports for the President's Award this year, and won. That's why my **position** is that Yolanda should be accepted into the program."

2. **The Classic STAR Model.** Although frequently used for behavioral interviewing, the STAR Model is great for staying on track when telling a more in depth story or situation.

   ° Situation: What was the high level situation?
   ° Task: What did you need to do in terms of the challenges and tasks?
   ° Action: What did you actually do?
   ° Result: What was the impact?

I'll give you a short example:

"(Situation) My department was struggling to stay within its budget limitations. (Task) I needed to come up with a way to cut costs and save money for the company. (Action) I pulled my team together and we started a competition where people could submit cost cutting and revenue building ideas, and the best ideas would be implemented right away. (Result) We ended up coming in under budget, and the people who generated the best ideas got a day off with pay."

Once you learn these two basic models, you can begin to practice clear expression of your thoughts. If you have an upcoming presentation or meeting where you will be speaking, practice these models with the thoughts you want to share. Record your voice, or do a dry run with a friend or colleague until it feels more natural.

4. The Words You Speak.

Your choice of words influences your level of credibility.

Intelligence is not measured by how long or elaborate your words are, but how your words clarify an idea.

When we use words that people don't understand, it does *not* make us appear smarter. In fact, it alienates us from our audience. It's like talking in a foreign language and an interpreter is required. I've had conversations with people and have had to ask, "Can you say that with less words?" or "What I think you're saying is _____(my translation), is that correct?"

My first tip is to simplify your words so your message doesn't get lost. You can still throw in a big word here and there, but recognize that people just can't process an endless story of complexity.

Example: *"The dichotomy of our complicated processing center from a brain perspective exudes an opposing view of intellectual expression, and we are left to endless pontification of convoluted outputs that don't consider our idiosyncratic tendencies."*

Simplified: *"There are two ways the brain processes thoughts, and they look opposite of each other. These two types of expression don't take into account our individual uniqueness."*

We sometimes use words or phrases to soften our responses in order to appear agreeable. I call these "qualifiers", and they diminish our credibility. Qualifiers are commonly used, especially when we feel insecure. Those who are uncomfortable with confrontation also use them to indirectly express their true message. Here are examples of what they look like:

- ° *"I think we should stop the project now, unless, of course, you feel like we should move forward."*
- ° *"I'm not trying to overstep my bounds, but do you believe that's the right approach?"*
- ° *"I'm not an expert, like you, on this topic, but maybe we should allow everyone to take a survey so we can get their feedback."*

Some other words that fit into the qualifier category include:

- ° Sort of
- ° Kind of
- ° A bit of
- ° But
- ° Sometimes
- ° I don't know, maybe

You don't have to banish all these words from your dictionary forever, but I suggest you learn to limit the use of them. A person with strong presence uses words of certainty. Compare the following two statements. Which one demonstrates confidence?

"I sort of want to review the presentation before you give it. I don't know, what do you think?"

"I would like to review the presentation before you give it. What are your thoughts on the matter?"

The first statement makes me think you are scared and unsure, and it leads me to eventually not trust your judgment. The second statement is much more solid and sure, and you are still inviting me into the conversation.

Another way we can increase our credibility through words has to do with lowering our use of acronyms.

Our world is so overwhelmed with information and we've resorted to shortened symbols to help us deal with it. Organizations are well known for collapsing complicated concepts into 3 or 4 letter shortcuts. I personally think acronyms are a wonderful invention. My favorite one is DWYSYWD, which means *Do What You Said You Would Do*. Unfortunately, the overuse of them can get old and annoying.

If you've ever started with a new company, you know you are in for a treat when you have to learn the cultural language. Imagine going into a meeting for the first time, and hearing this:

"We are giving a 3-up 3-down on the S.T.O.P. campaign started by our ILT Team so we can be compliant with OSHA and ACA."

Obviously, your head would be spinning with questions about what the campaign really is, and what ILT stands for.

The point is that you would lose the purpose of the meeting because you got hung up on letters. You might also feel like you're stupid, which could cause you to hold a little negativity toward the messenger.

You don't have to be new to a company to understand the challenge with using acronyms.

Our brains treat acronyms like zip files, so every time we hear one, our brain has to open all the files to process the meaning.

The process goes fairly quick, but it takes extra energy that keeps us from being fully focused.

The punch line here is that if you want the audience to understand you clearly, you should minimize your acronyms. Be mindful of those in the room who may not be familiar with them. Explain what they are so you can be respectful to everyone there.

5. The Sound of Your Voice.

The voice is your instrument to inspire, influence, and move your audience. You can play it boldly, or you can keep the tone soft. You can inflect to build interest and you can pause to capture immediate attention.

Everything you've done to build presence has led to this critical act of speaking aloud.

I like to get my coaching clients to record themselves in a personal video introduction and send it to me as part of our work together. Next, I get them into a conference room to record a presentation. I review the two videos to compare the difference in the voice elements and find that people are much more vocally energetic in their personal videos. It just goes to show that passion and confidence have a direct influence on how you use your voice. Finding ways to bring pieces of your overall story into the room will give you natural fuel that energizes others.

These are the elements to build skill in (and that means lots of practice in the car or in the bathroom):

1. **Volume.** The loudness of your voice can easily be used to have people sit up and take notice. High volume can create excitement and get the endorphins going. Lowering it softly right at the time you need to make a sensitive point can cause others to lean in and listen more closely. I would caution you to avoid using the same volume all the time. People get bored with you fast because it sounds like white noise (i.e. a constant fan blowing) and you end up lulling them to sleep.

2. **Pitch.** Do you have a high, mid-range, or low pitch voice? Whatever you are blessed with, you will want to create a range to express sound. Staying in the high range all the time can really become irritating for a listener, so practice visiting the mid-range to create interest. The same rule of thumb goes for a low pitch voice. Sometimes it can sound like the voice is breaking up, similar to a bad cold. Keep your voice smooth without crackliness (I realize this word isn't in the dictionary, but it fits). Keep the highs and lows to a minimum and only visit those vocal areas when you need to add flavor to your sound.

3. **Inflection.** When you put emphasis on certain words or parts of a sentence, we call this inflection.

Again, you are drawing attention to your voice and your message when you change it up. Look at the following sentences, noting that ALL CAPS means you emphasize by going down or up with your pitch. Take a moment to say these aloud:

- ° *"My hope is that today you will commit to working on your voice through dedicated practice, and because you want to be the bright bulb in the room."*
- ° *"My HOPE is that TODAY you will commit to working on YOUR VOICE through DEDICATED practice, and because you want to be the BRIGHT BULB in the room."*

Think about how inflection causes people to focus in on your meaning. It helps draw people into a mood or feeling. You want to use inflection with important words that you need people to really hear.

4. **Pausing.** The beauty of pausing is that it can be subtly dramatic, yet effective for giving people a moment to reflect on what was just said. If you have a critical point that you want to be remembered, pause right before it, or right after it. Another tip is when you are presenting, wait 7-8 seconds after you ask a question that you really want answered. It will feel like an eternity while you are waiting, but worth it to get people to interact with you. Introverts take longer to process so they will appreciate the extra time.

5. **Diction.** This element is important because it highlights the way we pronounce our words, our

consonants, and syllables. You can think of diction as being like a camera and the focus of its lens. Those who are good at this speak with tight and clear pronunciation and are in sharp focus. Those of us who struggle may skip over letters or hurry through it, which projects a blurry picture of words. I sometimes catch myself leaving the "g" off words like *going* and *doing* (goin' and doin'), which is a diction issue. I'm working on it.

6. ***Tone.*** The tone of your voice sends signals to others about the meaning of your words and influences the feeling in the room. It can be friendly, fearful, anxious, foreboding, or exhilarating. You actually have a lot at stake with HOW you say your words, and it impacts your personal brand. Have you ever had someone approach you with questions like:

   ○   *"What did you mean by saying that?"*
   ○   *"I picked up that you weren't happy with the results, are you okay?"*
   ○   *"I could tell you wanted to jump up and down in a victory dance!"*

   These are an indication that you're nonverbally giving a certain message. We don't always talk about it, but it's there. My position is that tone is fueled by internal strengths and challenges. I've witnessed people whose personal issues unintentionally showed up in their tone. Despite efforts to cover up true feelings, we become transparent to our audience whether we are feeling positive or if we're having a rough go of it. Consider this request for coaching on presentation skills with slightly different tones:

a) *"Would you be willing to work with me on my presentation skills?"*
b) *"Help me with my presentation skills."*
c) *"I suck at presentation skills. (sigh)"*
d) *"You are great at presentation skills. What can you teach me?"*
e) *"I was told I need to work on presentation skills and I was given your number."*

Each sentence has a unique tone that tells the listener about you. What message is each sentence sending? Here's what I hear:

a) *"I am humbly requesting your help and I want to learn."*
b) *"I'm a bit desperate, there's no time for niceties."*
c) *"I have a negative and self-defeatist attitude, and I'm too proud to ask."*
d) *"I'm excited by your skill and would love you to be my teacher!"*
e) *"I'm reluctant and not really happy about this. I'm doing it because I am being pressured."*

Think about the tones you use with people. Which ones are serving you well, and which ones do you need to work on? It's really a conscious choice to shape your message and bring certain energy to the dialogue without letting any personal issues shine through. Working on *you* isn't a singular event. You'll find that you need to continually grow and develop to keep yourself free of toxic emotions and thoughts.

These 5 Influencers are powerful pieces of your executive presence, and you can build skill through planning and practice.

All 5 Influencers feed into an important outcome: how people feel as a result of your presence.

Does your presence empower others, or does it minimize them? Do your words build up, or tear down a person's worth? Do your expressed thoughts activate inspiration, or provoke confusion? Executive presence is highly emotional, and the 5 Influencers are funnels to the feelings of your audience. Invest in personal work and development here.

My biggest recommendation is that you get in front of a camera or use your phone to practice and review your style. Once a week, get in your car alone and record a conversation. This is really effective when you are preparing to lead a meeting, or you know you are going to have a high stakes conversation with someone. You will quickly see and hear how others might be taking in your presence so you can take immediate action.

I personally put this recommendation into practice for myself, and it's how I discovered that was overusing the word *so*. I instantly went on a mission to reduce the number of times I spoke that word. Now, I only say it 3 times a day, rather than a hundred times a day.

Don't stop there. Get an accountability partner involved who can give you a different perspective and some needed inspiration. This person should be someone you trust and will really have your best interest at heart. You will be glad that you've gotten an outside opinion.

CHAPTER 6

Your New Definition of Executive Presence

his might be the shortest chapter on the planet. You get to finish it by crafting your unique definition of executive presence. Hopefully you've done your homework and have a list of key words or phrases to use for our next step.

A definition is a result of ingredients that have been creatively blended together. Anyone who's ever baked a cake knows that you have to add frosting (or some other kind of topping) for the cake to be complete. So, that's what we are going to do, metaphorically speaking.

If you recall, we put together a baseline definition of executive presence:

The power of an authentic human being to confidently put plans and actions into effect.

I have my own personal definition that works for me because it gets to the essence of everything we've looked at so far in the book. Here it is:

The power of an authentic person to confidently put plans and actions into effect by showing up in a way that he/she is seen, heard, valued, and celebrated.

It's time to add your topping to the cake. As you look at your list, think about what concepts, key phrases, or words jump out at you. What is really important to you about what you've captured? Is it about being the bright bulb in the room? How about a personal value you identified, like integrity or freedom? Let's try on some of the words and experiment. Here are a few to inspire you:

The power of an authentic human being to confidently put plans, actions, or laws into effect while practicing integrity, freedom, and candor.

The power of an authentic person to be a bright bulb in the room by putting plans, actions, or laws into effect with confidence and emotional intelligence.

The power of an authentic person to go from invisible to incredible by confidently putting plans, actions, or laws into effect, and to show up you.

Now it's your turn. Craft as many as definitions as you want then let them sit for a day or two. Come back to them and narrow your brainstorm down to one that truly fits you. This is the one time you don't have to go seek feedback because this definition belongs to YOU, and only you know who you are inside and out. This is the *secret of executive presence*. Your authenticity brings presence to fruition.

Are you ready to reveal your secret by declaring your definition of executive presence? You can let the world know by posting it at www.schoolofexecutivepresence. com then start your new journey of personal evolvement and freedom to *show up you*. I wish you much success and can't wait to hear from you on your progress.

PART II

Executive Presentation

A VEHICLE FOR EXECUTIVE PRESENCE

Presence and presentation are inexplicably tied together. Some would vehemently oppose me on this point, but here's the truth of the matter: presentations are a major vehicle for executive presence to manifest itself. Sometimes that is your *5 minutes of fame.* If you don't show up with incredible command of the room, you will be another timeslot on the executive agenda. Conversely, if you show up brilliantly but you don't have structure, your credibility plummets. This is the mother of all first impressions.

If you've ever watched the popular entrepreneur investment reality show *Shark Tank* you will have seen the marriage of presence and presentation coming to fruition (or not). I've witnessed charismatic people totally blow their pitch because they were relying upon their charm and good looks to get financial backing. Others obviously worked hard on the presentation, but forgot to bring their authenticity and confidence to the table.

The people who get *the sharks* to buy into what they're selling strike a balance of presence and presentation. In case you don't know who *the sharks* are, they are multi-billion dollar gurus with lots of money to invest in other people's ideas. They also stand to gain (or lose) on their investment, so the idea, person, and presentation have to be phenomenal. You will want create your presentations and meetings with this in mind.

Case in point: Max Gunawan, an intelligent and unassuming entrepreneur, stood in front of the sharks to present a mesmerizing product called *Lumio.* The portable product, a stunning and beautiful light in the form of a book, opened in accordion style to create a radiant light without the hindrance of cords.

Max's style was calm, stealth, and credible. He didn't have to make it all flashy and loud to sell the concept, he simply had to show up as himself. He did all of the things we talked about in part 1 of this book, and he nailed it. The structure of his presentation was a work of art as he elegantly painted his vision: *"I want this to live in your bag."*

I told my husband as we watched it all unfold, *"I want that!"* I also haven't forgotten the way Max showed up so powerfully. Incidentally, my husband bought the *Lumio* light for me on Mother's Day, so now I have a powerful reminder. When I see the light, I am reminded that *anyone* can be a bright bulb in the room.

The idea, person, and presentation are the ingredients you need to go from common to compelling.

Let's get going.

CHAPTER 1

Introduction to the Fine Dining Delivery Method™

*Y*ou enter the restaurant and are immediately enveloped by sophistication and succulent aromas. Your senses are tickled by anticipation as you scan the room. It's a clean and crisp picture of beautifully designed fixtures with strategically positioned lighting. There, in the center of the room, is your table. This will be an experience never to be forgotten.

You don't even have a chance to wonder if someone will be attending to you because he's already there, pouring your water and presenting you with a choice of the finest wines to get you started on your evening. He shares the menu choices with you and gives you a few moments to mull over the meal plan. He hurries away to expedite your wishes.

The appetizer arrives and is stunning in appearance. It's so lovely that you hate to disturb this piece of art, but you are hungry. You devour it and it's left you wanting more. Just when you can't stand it, another exquisite display of beauty arrives as your main course.

You approach this dish with respect because you want to absorb the flavors. Hurrying would be a missed opportunity. You discover as you are eating that there's a momentary loss of control and you have to slow yourself down again. By the end of the course, you are slightly full, but not saturated.

As you bask in the memory of the meal, your table host is back with a gorgeous dessert. You react with emotion. "Oh my! I really shouldn't be eating this! But I will. (Happy sigh)" You now feel whole. The check comes, and it is worth every dollar. This was a fantastic investment.

Have you ever had a true fine dining experience? Chances are you have, and it left a permanent impression. Think about how it impacted you. You probably have an equally memorable experience of going to a big buffet and exploding with regret afterwards. Turn your attention to *this* type of experience:

You walk into Barney's Buffet and are greeted by the cook/cashier, who's sporting a grease-stained apron with pizza sauce. Yummy!

"Seat yourself," he says, as he points to the dining area, where several tables have yet to be bussed from recently departed customers. You shrug your shoulders and overlook it. After all, you are pretty hungry.

You grab your plate from the rack and head over to the buffet where 3 varieties of fried chicken are sitting. You also encounter a pizza bar, fried fish, French fries, and more fried stuff. It seems like miles of fattening foods are already clogging your arteries as if the oil is floating in the air attaching itself to you.

You sit down and start cramming it in. Half way in, you are already full. Maybe if you put that plate aside and try something else, it will get better. You get a second plate of food, but it seems to have similar flavors—grease with a side of meat. You give up and go to the dessert bar, where you find factory processed brownies, cakes, and pies. You end up trying them all so you can justify how much you spent on the buffet.

At the end of it all, you are ridiculously full and miserable. Why did you eat all of that? You now have indigestion and feel sick as you recall how much you paid. Was it worth it? You decide the answer is NO. You probably need to go take a nap now.

Executive presentations can be equated to the Fine Dining Experience™ and the buffet style delivery.

The buffet style of presentation overloads the audience with too much information and fluff. There's not much organization or structure to it, and it definitely puts people to sleep. Sadly, tons of executive presentations tend to fall into the buffet category. If we are honest with ourselves, many of us are guilty of it.

The Fine Dining Experience™ is a well thought out plan and gives the audience just enough to make them want more. It evokes emotion while presenting structure. At the end, our attention is held and a positive and memorable impression is created.

As we begin our journey on how to build presentations, I want to share valuable nuggets of information to help shape your work more effectively. We'll also get into more detail on these topics once we start working with the presentation structure.

Our goal? Create a Fine Dining Experience™. Let's start with the basics.

CHAPTER 2

What You Need to Know About Delivering Executive Presentations

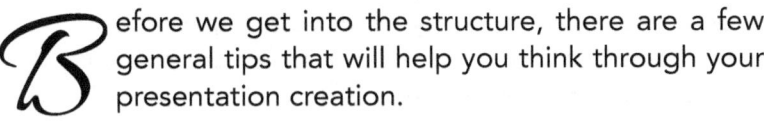efore we get into the structure, there are a few general tips that will help you think through your presentation creation.

CREATE THE STORY FIRST, THEN THE SLIDES

Imagine you are standing in a long hall and you see a door at the other end. Your goal is to get through that door. On each side of the hallway are several doors, and as you walk toward your goal, you find yourself going into each and every room. You start scavenging, and you believe you have to explore every nook and cranny. After all, you just might need some extra "tools" to get you through the door.

Pretty soon, you lose track of time. If and when you finally reach the door, you are overloaded with bags of stuff, and you can't get through the door. The opportunity is lost.

I call this going down the dark hall of PowerPoint.

How many of us are guilty of opening a blank slide template, starting to build from the first slide, and adding as we go? We get to the end, and those of us who love lots of detail sprinkle in laborious data because we think every dot and tittle is important. You can equate this ineffective strategy to going into every single door of the dark hall of PowerPoint; therefore causing your presentation to be saturated with so much data that others are exhausted by the time you get to the end of the hallway.

Everyone knows that slide shows are the accepted form of communication in the corporate world. The biggest mistake people make in their preparation is to use slides, instead of the story, to drive the presentation. It's a misnomer to think that PowerPoints are the easy way to present when they actually make the situation more complicated.

Your audience needs to get to the door. I'm going to show you how to get there by creating your story first then how to use slides to complement it. You may even be a risk taker and choose not to use slides at all. For now, let's address the attention span of your audience.

ATTENTION SPAN OF THE AUDIENCE

Our brains tire easily. Researchers like Dianne Dukette, David Cornish (2009), and James Cutting, a psychologist at Cornell University, generally say that you can only pay attention for so long before you have to do something else. Some experts say 20 minutes is all you have; others say 6-8 minutes in a presentation setting is the norm. I've found that it's even less than that in an executive presentation. Our first graph shows the declining attention span of the average person.

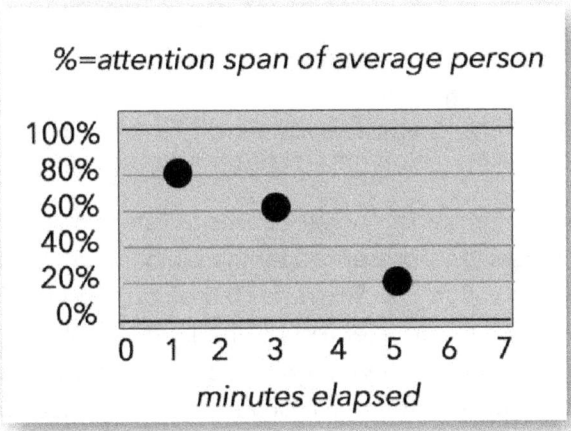

What we find is that attention starts to decline within the first minute, and we go from 100% to 80% in our focus. At 5 minutes, attention is falling to 20%. In fact, lack of attention begins to snowball rapidly if you haven't captured your audience's attention quickly.

It's a fact that you have to engage your audience effectively within the first 8 seconds, or the attention span drops even more dramatically.

Our next graph shows what happens to the attention span in an executive level presentation.

Also:

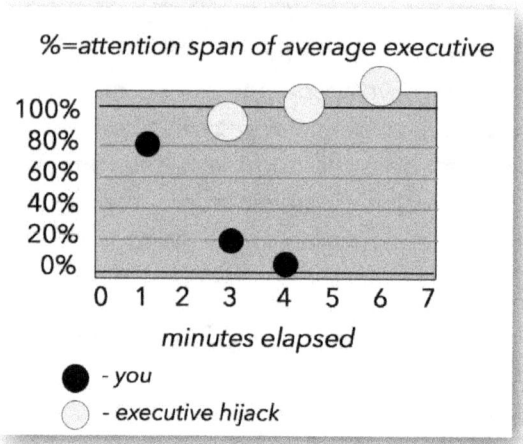

There's a tendency for executives to listen to you for a couple of minutes (as represented by the black dots), the *hijack* the presentation within 2 to 5 minutes if their attention isn't powerfully captured, as represented by the lighter color dots. Most high-level leaders are dealing with mental filters that lower their focus on your presentation. Many are overwhelmed with problems that we may not be privy to, and their brains are jumping around trying to find answers. Don't take it personally; just be aware that this is what you are dealing with.

If you have a data rich presentation, you want to tell a story about it (versus a million bullet points) to keep it memorable because stories hold attention longer.

This might require you to have data in the form of a supplemental document that you've sent before or after the meeting. We'll explore further what to put in and what to leave out as we move into *The Fine Dining Delivery Method™* part of the book.

This brings us back to slides. Keep them to a minimum, preferably around 5 slides. You may have just gasped, but trust me when I say you won't get much further than that in a 30-60 minute presentation because of attention span. You can create 10, but you will find yourself skipping around to fit the information they are looking for.

You want them to remember YOU, not just the data, so avoid the side doors in the dark hall of PowerPoint.

PLANNING YOUR TIME

It's a rare occurrence for anyone to get through an entire presentation exactly as planned. Here is an important rule of thumb:

Plan to deliver in half the time you are allotted.

If you have a 10-minute presentation, plan to deliver it as if you only had 5 minutes. If you have a 60-minute presentation, plan for 30. The longer the presentation, the more you will have to incorporate shifts of attention to keep it alive. This means you have to start creating some type of interaction, dialogue, or activity. Inviting others in takes up time, leaving less time for you.

APPEALING TO ALL TYPES OF LEARNERS

My friend, Bob Bennett, and I agree strongly that you have to appeal to all types of people when you present. The former Chief Learning Officer for FedEx for many years and author of *"Leadership is (Dot, Dot, Dot)"*, Bob identifies 5 categories of learners in his own words:

- ° **The *"What"* People** want to clarify the issues and understand the problem. "What is it? What does it look like? What do we need to know?"
- ° **The *"How"* People** want the answers so they can fix the situation. "How will we tackle this? How will it get done?"
- ° **The *"Touchy Feely"* People** want relationship motivation, and inspiration. "How will this connect me to others? Who will this help? How will it help me fulfill my mission?"
- ° **The *"Implication"* People** want to understand the impact of actions and decisions. "Why should we do this? What will it give us? What will it take away from us?"
- ° **The *"What If"* People** want to play out all the possibilities. "What if we don't succeed? What if we start tomorrow? What if we waited?"

Bob's general synopsis on how to get your message across to everyone is a good one.

"You have to relate to them by understanding the past, the present, and future relationship. Ask yourself what your scope is. You don't want to tackle changing the world, so you really have to define the space. Once you do that, you have to hone in on cause and effect, which requires some self-education on the problem. Once you know the problem, be prepared to bring solutions rather than more problems or complaints. You will definitely need some numbers in your presentation, which

quantifies substance. I also like to use metaphors, they are memorable and tend to really stick with people."

The moral of the story is: If you don't bring a solution, you don't bring value.

LEARNING STYLES IN PRESENTATION

The learning style of your audience is equally important to consider. This may be old news to you, but I have to call it out as a point of consideration. We go more in-depth on this topic in *The School of Executive Presence™*, but for the purpose of the book, we will stick with the basic facts.

- º People fall into three categories when it comes to style preference:
- º *Auditory:* Learns by hearing (Tell Me)
- º *Visual:* Learns by seeing (Show Me)
- º *Kinesthetic:* Learns by doing (Let Me Do It)

Most people have a dominant style, so when you are presenting, you can best engage everyone when you use all three. I want to stress that you are there to participate at an executive level, so be careful to not turn the presentation into a workshop. Getting your audience to do something might mean inviting them in with questions, or having them participate in a demonstration.

The majority of presentations are boring to people because they tend to be geared toward the auditory learner.

Auditory learners only make up about 10-15% of the entire population. The only thing that keeps visual learners engaged is the graphics on slides or your animated appearance, and they equal about 40% of your audience. The rest are kinesthetic, so a big opportunity exists to DO something with them. I should note that visual learners have to see you first before they hear you. If they like what they see, they will listen.

Brilliant presentations appeal to all three styles.

In the next chapter, we'll explore the three types of presentation that these styles all respond to, so keep that in mind as you read.

CHAPTER 3

The Three Types of Presentation

*P*eople who are tactical will love this part of the book. I know you want to get to the nuts and bolts, so we are going to turn down the volume on reflective inspirations and move on to practicality. This means we'll focus on the "what, how, and sometimes why" of executive presentation.

Let's look at three types of presentations that are generally used in business:

- ° *Inform:* providing data, giving updates, educating
- ° *Persuade:* you want something and you need help from the audience

    °   *Celebrate:* you are sharing stories, successes, and creating relationships

Each one requires a slightly different approach when presenting, so it's important to understand the purpose of each one.

INFORM

Most presentations are designed to share an important piece of information. This could be an update on a project, or the status of how well a product or service is going. You could be there to educate the audience about an event that's happening or teach them how to work through a process.

My first tip is to open up the informational presentation with a short and sweet statistic to capture attention right away. An example might be:

"A global IBM study of 1500 CEOs revealed the number one competency needed for the future of business. Do you know what it is? Creativity."

Make sure it is direct, relevant to your topic, and truly informative.

Even when you are just sharing, you also want something from the audience. Are you seeking to build a relationship with them? Are you hoping for credibility affirmation? Are you being collaborative because you'll need help somewhere down the line?

I'm saying that you don't just inform people because it's the nice thing to do, that's just dry and boring. Think about you're really trying to achieve. What is your purpose? You will want to integrate this purpose into the presentation and create a call to action because leaders are achievers. If they don't have skin in the game or have to DO something, they will tune you out. Here's an example of how you go from boring to brilliant:

Boring:

"I'm here to tell you about the product launch and how it's going."

Brilliant:

"I'm going to share what's been happening on the product launch, and I invite you to look at the data and test it. We all support the same mission; my goal is to hear you and move on your suggestions."

The second response brings your audience into your world and ties you to each other. You want to appeal to their heads and hearts while inviting them into a common cause with you.

When you only provide information, you leave out the heart part, and they can't connect to you emotionally.

PERSUADE

You need something and you can't get it without the audience. That's the gist of a persuasive presentation. You might be trying to sell an idea like on *Shark Tank*, or you may need sponsorship for your nonprofit organization. It doesn't matter if the end game is a tangible item or you are looking for leadership support for your initiative, you have to appeal to *emotions* and *logic* while *managing your presence* well.

People end up flopping when they rely too heavily on one of these three ingredients. Too much data is overkill, and too much touchy feely lingo makes everyone uncomfortable. Storytelling is a great approach, and you only need one main story to capture attention.

If you kick off your presentation with a very brief story or a thought provoking question then move into your data, you will connect with people sooner.

The key is to weave tiny parts of your story in throughout, and end with a data summary, call to action, and story finalization. Here's an example of an opener:

"Imagine the workplace several years from now. A place where CEOs are elected, not appointed. Social responsibility is a performance measure. Your office is your mobile device. (Pause). This is the future of the workplace, are we ready for it?"

"I want to show you how we can increase our engagement and productivity by 20%, reinvent our business, and meet the demands of this inevitable future workplace in a way that will grow our profitability by at least 10% each year."

You've just created usable material to cushion the blow of needing budget money. You need to be transparent about the upside and downside of your proposal. If there is a major hurdle to overcome, introduce it early so your audience can work through the change cycle and begin trusting you early. Here's what you might say:

> *"I estimate this will cost $800,000 to accomplish. It's a big amount. I have researched some creative ways we can soften the blow. Let's look at the data so we can understand what it will take..."*

You will likely face immediate opposition.

You've introduced a shocking fact or request. Your audience is now faced with a change, and you are going to help them through it. In case you aren't familiar with the change cycle, it's a normal process we all go through when we get new information. There are four stages:

1. **Deny.** *"This isn't happening,"* or *"This is the flavor of the month, it'll go away."*
2. **Resist.** *"I don't like this and I want to fight it. I know it's real but if I push hard enough it will die down."*
3. **Explore.** *"I guess this is really happening. I need to learn more about it."*
4. **Accept.** *"I am on board. What can I do to help?"*

The smartest move is to connect with your audience members *before* you ever enter the room so they know what to expect, but that isn't always possible. You will still have to get them used to your idea, so don't hold the bad news until the end. It will be like a punch in the face and you will lose credibility. Bring them back to the story and the result you plan to get:

> *"When we follow the path I've shown you, it will lead us to a future where employees are giving their full discretionary effort. We will be leading the pack on innovative work practices, and we'll have a few extra million in the bank account."*

This type of presentation takes strategy, solid research, and methodical planning, so take your time to develop it and practice with a trusted friend or colleague before you get in front of decision-makers.

CELEBRATE

Celebratory and inspirational presentations are a good fit for feel-good occasions, but don't underestimate the power they have to build your brand and persuade. Of the three types of presentation, this one evokes vulnerability. You have permission to turn up the volume on personal stories, and turn down the dial on data (but not completely down).

The results are important to know but the impact of the results is the critical factor.

We love victorious stories and personal accounts of overcoming circumstances because they bring the possibility of success for others. The inspirational or celebratory presentation is that message of hope people need as fuel to go on with their goals and dreams. It can also spark inspiration to make changes or start a new path.

One of the most effective approaches I've seen involves an introductory video or personal life-changing testimony that kicks off the celebration. People want to experience that moment when the situation goes from "We didn't know if we were going to make it," to "The pivotal moment was when _____ happened, and then we came out on top as rock stars."

After your audience burns with initial excitement, joy, or empathy, the question becomes, "How did you really accomplish this?" If you say, "Oh we just had some great luck," you will automatically kill your credibility and water down the success. This is where you have to bring in logic, a little data, and a dash of sparkle.

I was hosting an end of year celebration for our first graduating class of a corporate talent discovery program. The milestone was a great victory because, fourteen months earlier, I promised my risk-adverse leader that this experimental program would work.

About three months in, my team and I were already seeing the benefits, and small wins started to surface. By the end of the program we had achieved above and beyond what everyone expected, and the accolades from senior leaders were rolling in. I knew I had to show everyone in the room how and why it worked.

I created a minimalist profile of each participant with their picture, their main goal, and their biggest success at the end. I created a 2-minute video with these profiles and added some music, "Pump Up The Jams". After it played, a room full of participants, their colleagues, and the company leaders erupted into applause. I waited until the room became quiet then shared actual statistics of how the participants progressed, had built relationships with leaders, moved into new positions, and became much more productive for the business.

The end of the celebration was equally important, and I closed with the story of my first conversation with my leader, revealing the process of getting approval to run the program. My team and I expressed our gratefulness to my leader, and it was a powerful time. People left the room as believers. We didn't even have to ask if the program would be funded again.

When you seek to inspire or celebrate, be thinking about gratefulness, data, and intention. If you incorporate these things, you'll build a more memorable brand that people will want more of.

We are now ready to focus on the structure of our Fine Dining Delivery Experience™ so we can deliver a brilliant presentation.

CHAPTER 4

Structure – Planning the "Meal"

We begin with *the big picture of a fine dining executive presentation.* You can think of this component as the *meal planning*, which includes 4 areas of focus:

- ° *Determining the overall goal*
- ° *Formulating the 3 main points*
- ° *Knowing the audience and their needs*
- ° *Engaging the audience with interaction and action*

DETERMINING THE OVERALL GOAL

The biggest message: You will most likely feel the pressure to hurry up your presentation, and time will go fast. Think about what would cause you to be satisfied. To boil down your goal, ask yourself these questions:

- ° What do I want this presentation to do?
- ° What do I want the people in the room to do as a result?
- ° What is the big message that has to be shared?
- ° What is the one thing that matters by the time it's all said and done?

Type of presentation: We spent time looking at the three kinds of presentations. Is your goal to *inform, persuade,* or *celebrate*? Review Chapter 3 to ensure you're clear on how each type should be approached.

FORMULATING THE 3 MAIN POINTS

Once you clearly define your main goal, it's time to break it down into 3 main points, and *only* 3 points. The fact is that people cannot retain much beyond that, so we need to stay in step with the Fine Dining Experience™ versus the buffet.

Let's say that you are creating a *persuade style* presentation, and your main goal is to gain approval to launch a new product line for the business. Your three points might be around these topics:

1. The benefits of the product line itself.
2. The potential challenges of the launch.
3. What the return on investment will be.

Your points should be leading the audience full circle to the goal in the form of a request, action, or result.

KNOWING THE AUDIENCE AND THEIR NEEDS

Timing: Remember the rule of planning to deliver in half the time you are allotted. Executives like to process things aloud and in the moment, so prepare to boil down your main points. It's a rarity to be asked, *"How much time do you need?"* It's more likely you will be given a set amount of time to present, which usually ranges between 20 and 60 minutes.

Prioritize your points in order of importance, and plan to re-emphasize them at the end of your presentation. Time your most important point as closely as you can to the beginning of your presentation, and reinforce it at the end.

Knowledge level: Determine how much your audience already knows, and what is truly important for them to know. This is where we get into trouble with the *dark hall of PowerPoint*, and we think we have to share all the details. Don't make the room work hard to wade through the weeds. It's better to share a big idea and have them ask questions versus starting with a tiny detail and working your way up to the idea. Your audience will get impatient fast.

If at all possible, send them a short synopsis of what you plan to discuss before the presentation. The ideal scenario is to get on any of your audience's calendar to get their feedback before you step in front of them. Another option is to review the information with someone from the next level down to bounce your presentation off them.

Personal and Professional Intel: Look for ways to connect and form relationships with your executives. At minimum, you should understand their role in the organization, and any current challenges they are facing.

- ° Are they leading a particular initiative or company change?
- ° What successes have they experienced recently?
- ° Do you potentially have a solution to a problem they have?

On a personal level, try to learn what their interests are. These are topics of conversation that can break the ice or bring about a point you may have.

- ° Does someone like a particular sport, like football?
- ° Is someone a volunteer at the local boys and girls club?
- ° Does someone have triplets?

One time I was meeting with my vice president about an open position on my team. My preferred candidate was a strong performer and expert in the field, but my VP argued that we should fill the position with a *high potential* individual who could move into leadership.

My position was that I already had two *high potential* people on my team. I needed to find a way to reach this leader so she would hear me. Finally, it occurred to me that she was a football fan.

"I appreciate your perspective, but I already have two quarterbacks. I need a linebacker to fill this position."

Boom! That got her attention and resonated with her personal interests. She smiled and said she couldn't argue with that reasoning. I gained agreement to move forward with my candidate.

Engaging the audience with interaction and action

You're in the front of the room, and you want to maintain as much control as possible. Contrary to popular belief, one of the best ways to keep it on track is to invite your audience into the presentation. It's a mistake to glide through in hopes of nobody interrupting you. This is about establishing a relationship with your audience, and some dialogue is required.

Wise people plan the questions and actions they will use *before* the presentation. Here are some ideas that you can add to your plan:

°   **Ask a "Before I begin" question**

> Example 1: *"What's the most important piece of information you want to get out of this presentation today?"*

> Example 2: *"What can I do to help you maintain interest in the topic today?"*

- ° **Ask a close-ended question at different times**

  Example 1: *"How many of you are familiar with our latest stock prices?"*

  Example 2: *"Who would like to see our turnover rate go down?"*

- ° **Have them do something**

  Example 1: *"Take a moment to write down the name of the most influential mentor you ever had. (Pause) Now just imagine if you had the chance to be that same kind of mentor to someone else. It can happen if we move forward with adding this program to our budget for next year."*

  Example 2: *"Turn to the person sitting to your right. If we aren't able to turn this sales strategy around, what are the chances that the person you're looking at won't be here next year?"*

- ° **Check in with them (after you've made your main point)**

  Example 1: *"I've shared some powerful news with you just now. What's your immediate reaction?"*

Example 2: *"I want to stop talking for a moment and check in with you. Gary, how can we move forward with this plan?"*

PLANNING IS YOUR FRIEND

The assembly of your presentation will be simplified when you do the planning first. This is so much easier than going down the dark hall of PowerPoint. You are basically creating the outline, and the rest of your development will be a piece of cake.

CHAPTER 5

Structure – The "Appetizer"

*T*he appetizer serves as the opening of your presentation. If you recall, you've got about 8 seconds to capture the attention of your audience, and it has to be intriguing. 4 pieces make up your appetizer:

1. Give an appetizer statement.
2. Introduce yourself.
3. Do a high-level information share.
4. Transition with a question.

1. GIVE AN APPETIZER STATEMENT.

Appetizers cause you to want more—if they are presented correctly. Think about some of the characteristics when it is brought to the table.

- ° It's small
- ° It's fresh
- ° It's beautifully designed
- ° It takes a short amount of time to consume

These are the ingredients you'll want to mix into your opening statement. We alluded to some openers in Chapter 3, and it's a good idea to align them with the type of presentation you are delivering. The use of a quote, brief introduction to a story, a metaphor, or research fact are good places to start.

So, you don't want to tell a joke like, *"Why did the chicken cross the road?"* then move on to *"Let's talk about why the corporate responsibility initiative needs more funding."*

Your appetizer statement should be relatable to the presentation topic and to the audience.

Let's bring back the remembrance of authenticity. How do you create this opener in a way that is real? You have to feel passionately about it, and resonate with it. You also have to be thinking about the people in the room. What will hit home with them? Here are some examples:

Brief Story Example: *"Chloe Smith is a young girl who needs our help. She's been diagnosed with a disease that our medicine could potentially cure. We can save her life with our decisions today."*

Metaphor Example: *"Today, we are at the poker table, and this executive team serves as the dealer.*

I'm a player who wants to be dealt the best hand of cards so we can get our product on the market, and our competitor has to fold."

Quote Example: *"Great minds talk about ideas. Average minds talk about things. Small minds talk about other people. These are wonderful words from Eleanor Roosevelt. There are great minds in here today, and I want to get your ideas on how we can develop our people to be ready for the future workplace."*

Research Fact Example: *"Good morning. In a recent company survey, only 30% of our leaders were able to tie their role directly to the mission of our company."*

You may need more time to figure out the statement, so don't worry if you can't immediately produce one. If you get stuck, move on to the rest of your presentation development, then come back to it to build it out.

2. INTRODUCE YOURSELF.

The routine way of introducing ourselves goes something like this:

"Hi, I'm_____. I'm glad to be here."

If you want to show up well, do your appetizer statement first, and introduce yourself second. Here's what I mean using the research fact in our previous example:

"Good morning. In a recent company survey, only 30% of our leaders were able to tie their role directly to the mission of our company.

My name is _____, and I want to share this survey information with you."

Sometimes I get asked, *"Well what if they already know me?"*

I recommend always stating your name in the introduction, especially if someone else hasn't introduced you. If there's someone in the room who you don't know well, take the opportunity to succinctly tell them who you are and what you do. You'll want to be memorable, and you want them to remember your name, not just your face.

3. DO A HIGH LEVEL INFORMATION SHARE.

Once you introduce yourself, the next step is to give a general idea of what you will be sharing. You can go back to the three points you did in the meal planning. We'll keep using the leadership survey to maintain consistency. Here's one way you might introduce the information:

"I'd like to share 3 things with you. First, I'll go over the significant results of the survey to give you an idea of our leadership's mindset. Secondly, I want to discuss how we are addressing some of the feedback through

our existing programs. Finally, I would like to propose a way we can tackle the two biggest challenges as we move forward."

If the room seems overly talkative or challenging, you may benefit from letting them know how many slides you have. It might sound like this:

"I have 5 slides for you today. Here are the 3 things I will discuss..."

You are helping your audience to know what to expect, which accelerates the change cycle that they are going through with you.

This part doesn't have to be difficult. Keep it simple, direct, and under 30 seconds.

4. TRANSITION WITH A QUESTION.

The goal of asking a question at this juncture is to get a new angle on attention span. You may have asked a question as part of your appetizer, which is great. If you are already experiencing more dialogue than you want, you don't have to necessarily ask another question, but it doesn't hurt.

Use the question to maintain control AND to build rapport.

Here are some examples:

"By a show of hands, how many of you are not surprised that 70% of our leaders aren't connected to the mission?"

"Who would like to see our leadership hold employees more accountable?"

"What's the one thing you want to hear about by the end of the presentation?"

Asking questions engages people, and they will be more willing to hear what you have to say next. This is exactly what an appetizer is designed to do, get you prepared for the main course.

CHAPTER 6

Structure –The "Main Course"

$\mathcal{W}$hat is the purpose of a main course? The meal is meant to satisfy your hunger, and it's the substance that your audience can't live without.

The best Fine Dining Experience™ is one that is balanced and lean.

When you develop your 3 points, ask yourself the following questions:

- ° What is the substance they can't live without?
- ° What is important about it?
- ° What data supports it?
- ° What action (if any) needs to be taken?

This will help you filter out things that could be considered *fluff and fat.*

BUILD YOUR POINTS

Let's use 1 of our 3 points from the previous chapter to build upon. Think about the questions above then start jotting down possible ideas to build upon.

Example:
1. Reveal the most significant data in the leadership survey results.

- ° Identify the top 3 strengths identified, and the 3 top weaknesses
    - ° Create smart graphs to simplify the results for my visual audience
    - ° Call out any anomalies like a high result in a particular department
- ° Highlight that leaders were asked how their role supports the company mission, 70% responded, "I don't know."
    - ° Identify possible reasons for this result
    - ° Ask the room what their reaction is or give them three reasons to choose from
- ° Stress that action is needed to address the survey results
    - ° Identify ideas your team has brainstormed
    - ° Identify the dollar cost of not addressing the mission problem

PRIORITIZE AND TRIM THE FAT

Once you go through all of your main points and brainstorm out ideas, go back and *trim the fat.* You can do this easier if you prioritize each point. Which one is most important? Which one is the lesser of the two?

Your biggest priority should be allotted the most time. It's like the meat of your presentation.

I always find it helpful to chunk the presentation out, something like this:

Point 1:   Leadership Survey Results - **Priority #1-10 minutes**
Point 2:   How we're addressing feedback - **Priority #3-5 minutes**
Point 3: How to tackle the biggest challenges - **Priority #2-7 minutes**

The other two points are like your side dishes, so those are the pieces you really want to look at trimming down.

CREATE THE STORY

You have your information together, now it's time to develop your story.

Create a story, not a bunch of bullet points.

You need to have a good understanding of your presentation, and reduce the amount of verbiage you are putting on the slides. Bullet points take the attention away from you; so don't allow them to compete.

This is a chance for you to be creative by using a metaphor, a character, testimonials, or integrating the audience's interests into the story. If you were thinking brilliantly and started this in your appetizer, you simply need to thread it through your presentation.

Here's an example metaphor for our leadership survey presentation:

> *"As you see, we have leaders here without a clear mission. It's like having them all in a life raft on the ocean, and they are all paddling in different directions. Can you imagine how exhausted they are? They need a compass."*

People remember you through the stories long after the presentation has come and gone.

Example 2

Let's walk through another example. This time, we are presenting about a product launch.

Let's pretend that our product line is called the Magic House Clutter Remover (something I would like to learn more about!). Here are 3 points with 3 data pieces for each one.

1. **The benefits of the Magic House Clutter Remover.**
    a. *Designed to reduce clutter in your cabinets, drawers, and closets.*

    b. *Ideal for business people with busy lives by saving time.*

    c. *Great value for the customer at a price of $59.99*

2. The potential challenges of the launch.

    a. *Recent issues on production line-inconsistent product output.*

    b. *Cost that is being incurred by a particular supplier is higher than expected.*

    c. *Delays due to decisions are sitting at the executive level.*

3. The Return on Investment.

    a. *Customers will be repeat buyers every month.*

    b. *Brand recognition will go viral.*

    c. *Opportunity to expand product line with upsells.*

In this example, we've identified our 3 focal points, and each point has 3 data pieces. I want to stress this warning: don't deceive yourself by cramming a hundred pieces of data under each point. Presenting everything in 3's is a great combination that prevents everyone from getting bogged down in mind draining data. Give 3 data pieces for each of the 3 points and build your story around this information so the presentation points will stick.

You have to think in terms of the story type messages now. It's better to have the minutia in your back pocket and have them ask you questions, as opposed to you loading them down with nonessential information that they would never even think of asking you. You are basically inviting them to interact with you, which is a fine dining tactic. The buffet style interaction doesn't invite conversation, nor does it draw your audience in because you are overloading them and they just want the presentation to be over.

There are so many ways this presentation could be developed from a story perspective. Here are some questions to spark your creativity:

- Could a real person or real story be infused into the data?
- Could you create fictional characters with memorable names to get your points across?
- Could you create a scenario using the people in the room?

Here is a courageous way to invite your audience into the storyline:

"I would like to share why Arnold, our Business Development Vice President, will be excited about going home today. He is experiencing the power of the Magic House Clutter Remover, a remarkable product designed for busy professionals who believe in living clean and clutter free. Not only is Arnold saving valuable time because of the Magic House Clutter Remover, he is saving money and the hassle of hiring a personal organizer. At a small investment of 59.99, Arnold is satisfied that his clutter is being cleared at the touch of a button thanks to this remarkable product."

You have just knocked out your 3 data pieces for the first point. For my more conservative readers, this may feel awkward and not your style. All is well, and you can create something that fits your authentic personality. It could sound like this:

"Today my wife will be really happy when I bring home the Magic House Clutter Remover. It will make her life- and

mine- much easier. At 59.99, who can complain? My issue is that I can't relax just yet because we have a challenge right now in production. I want to give you an update on what's happening and what needs to take place so I can get this fantastic product to my spouse so I can have a happy life, and our company can be on the road to business profitability."

You get the point.

Let's get ready to bring it all home with our last course, dessert.

CHAPTER 7

Structure – The "Dessert"

essert evokes strong emotion. It's also really sticky.

Our presentation ending should follow suit and the goal should be an inspirational call to action. Here's what needs to happen:

- ° Briefly summarize
- ° Bring the presentation full circle
- ° End on a high note (dessert)

BRIEFLY SUMMARIZE

Giving a 15-20 second summary is a good practice to have when presenting to executives. Some say it helps them remember what was discussed, but I personally think it sends a message to your audience that you are organized and have your stuff together. Your summary might sound something like this:

> "Today we've looked at the leadership survey results, I've shared some of the proactive measures we're taking to address the feedback in some of our existing programs, and we've looked at ways to address the main challenges."

It's that simple.

BRING THE PRESENTATION FULL CIRCLE

You'll want to ensure you have tied up any loose ends and identified any follow up actions that came up in the course of the presentation. If you got feedback at some point, be sure to respectfully thank everyone for sharing thoughts and ideas. Here's an example of how to bring it full circle:

> *"As a result of today, we'll move forward with the mission restart project, and I will follow up with each of you on the progress. Also, thanks so much for the feedback about our existing work. I will make the necessary adjustments by next Friday."*
>
> **This will be like boxing up the leftovers.**

END ON A HIGH NOTE

Finally, we come to the tastiest part of the dessert where we make it sticky.

What do you want to leave your audience with, a quote, a final play on the metaphor? Here are a couple of examples:

Example 1:

"I leave you with this thought. Give a man a paddle, and he'll use it. Give a man a mission, and he'll paddle harder. Give a man a compass, and he'll paddle harder in the right direction."

Example 2:

"Our time here has been good. Not just for me, but for the organization. Think about a year from now, where will we be? I imagine that our mission will be clearer than it's ever been, and our leaders will thank you for the support you demonstrated here. I am grateful."

Authenticity is key. You have to find the high note that taps into your passion and reveals the real you.

Occasionally, inspiration hits you while you are presenting. These defining moments invite risk. Go with it. The ending can invite lighthearted banter or a reminder of a memorable theme that popped up. Everything doesn't have to be scripted out. As a matter of fact, I encourage you to allow for some improvisation and vulnerability. Dessert evokes emotion so let some of that shine through.

CHAPTER 8

Life After the Presentation

SPOTLIGHT: WHEN IT ALL COMES TOGETHER

Joanna Martin is what I call "a bright bulb in the room". I met her through one of my talent discovery programs in 2013. From Day 1, she was a complete delight with positive energy. Here's what she has to say about her journey.

In 2012, I was re-evaluating what my next career steps should be. Honestly, I felt things were turning stagnate. I desperately searched for ways to get involved in our organization, network, and learn more. I wanted to take AND own my next steps. The opportunity came in spring 2013 as I was accepted into a new development program. Sitting in Orientation Day, I began comparing myself to the others.

"I don't measure up to these people!"

I couldn't believe what I had agreed to be part of. In time, however, I learned to not let my doubtful thoughts consume me. This was going to be the greatest opportunity I'd ever been provided in my career.

Over the next year, I had a team of peers and program leaders who inspired me, challenged me, and at times frustrated me. I was pushed out of my comfort zone by learning to receive and give both positive and constructive feedback on my presence in meetings, my presentation abilities, and my ideas.

I got to the place where I was able to leverage my strengths when meeting with people or speaking to leaders. I learned the Fine Dining Method of Executive Presentation, which was pretty eye opening for me. After all the workshops, networking events, and feedback sessions over the course of a year, I walked into our final presentation as a different individual than how I started—full of confidence, vibrant, and ready for the world! As I met one final time with my program mentor, I remember this feeling of "It's not over yet. You have so much to still give and share with others."

It was this point where I confidently stepped into my next role of Mentor. Two years ago, I would have never felt worthy enough to commit to this program, or even mentor another person. I was desperate to get involved, but terrified of not being good enough. Going through the process helped me to show up strong and step into the role I was called to do.

Now, I use what I've learned every day, whether I'm presenting in front of my peers, or to hundreds of individuals during a corporate town hall.

You are in one of two states of mind after a presentation: either basking in the glow of your success, or scrutinizing your performance and the things you forgot to do. You could also be replaying a rebuke you got from someone in the room.

BASKING IN THE GLOW

The feeling of success drives you to replay the experience over and over in your head. Others may be congratulating you and recognizing how well you did. You have a sense of pride and joy that you showed up with impact.

It's a time to be grateful. What are you thankful for? Who should you express this to? Don't let the experience stop here. Carry it through by communicating your gratefulness to the people who were in the room, but also let them know what actions you are taking. This is a chance to build the relationship outside of the room, so revisit PIES to think through how you can stay connected.

Be careful not to go overboard and turn into the executive stalker.

Send your *Thank You/I'm Grateful* note within two days of the presentation. Give it a couple of weeks then email (or share in person) any progress update or actions you are taking, but don't wait longer than 30 days for this second contact.

Don't be surprised if you don't get a response, or you get a very short response. If possible, see if you can provide a quarterly update to let everyone know how the project is coming along.

SCRUTINIZING YOUR PERFORMANCE

Did your presentation not go as well as you hoped?

You're probably thinking about the *afterthought* that showed up after you left the room. It's that super smart answer you wish you'd said in the moment that you really needed it. I encourage you to let it go.

If it were meant for you to express that thought, it would have happened.

If you found yourself stumbling during your presentation, or someone in the audience caught you off guard, consider yourself normal. Here's the deal: you had an experience. What went well? What did you learn? You have reason to celebrate if you gleaned something that you can use the next time.

When I help people deal with the aftermath of a less than perfect encounter, it usually surfaces that the presentation went better than they thought.

We beat ourselves up and apply our mental filters, blowing the negatives out of proportion. If we assess the situation appropriately, we find that the less effective presentations have been a result of:

- *Lack of preparation*
- *Losing your cool and becoming overly emotional*
- *Shutting down verbally when faced with adversity*

- ° Overkill on slides and/or data in lieu of connecting with the room
- ° Performing instead of authentically presenting

You have to ask yourself, "Did I fall into one of these scenarios?" If you did then you know what you need to work on.

Whatever you did or didn't do, you still need to move forward confidently with the *Thank You/I'm Grateful* note within two days of the presentation.

For the sake of the audience and yourself, MOVE ON.

THE EXECUTIVE REBUKE (STUN GUN)

In case you experienced the executive stun gun, welcome to the club!

You feel like you've had your head stomped in, but it's a pivotal learning moment and you need to get away by yourself and work through it. Time is a soothing source of healing, but you should also seek sources of encouragement. These may come in the form of a conversation with a close friend, purging your toxic thoughts through writing, or reading encouraging words.

Remember what we said in a previous chapter? Here it is in an abbreviated version:

Whatever is inside of a person comes out.

Refuse to take on other people's hang-ups, rather cling to the positive learning that you can use going forward. The experience is one that can be a lesson that you teach to others one day, just as I am teaching you now. You may not even be learning for your own sake, but to give back to those who come after you. Soak it in so you can give it back.

AT THE END OF THE DAY...

The check arrives. Was it worth it? If your audience got the Fine Dining Experience™, the answer is yes.

Acknowledgments

I always thought my first book would be a collection of my personal memoirs. But, I realized that a big part of my mission and message has been to my friends and colleagues in the business world. As I carried out the writing of this book, key individuals miraculously showed up at the perfect time.

I would like to first thank my husband, Aaron, whose raw critiques of my writing made me a better writer my first time around. Although sometimes his feedback had me cringing, he made me thoroughly think through what I wanted to say and portray. He certainly helped me to deliver quality content. For his honesty and love, I am deeply grateful for my sweetheart.

My oldest daughter, Jazmin Harper, is phenomenal at story structure analysis. I am grateful for her refreshing and positive encouragement when I first started writing. Jaz, I can't wait for your first book to be published!

Bob Bennett, thank you for the dialogue and your contribution to this book. You are the epitome of authentic leadership and executive presence. You inspire me.

Time is always a struggle for people in today's busy world, but my friend and colleague, Sarah Robinson, went out of her way to help me. In spite of her own busy schedule as a StrengthsFinder guru and consultant, she read through my manuscript with her professional eyes on and boosted my confidence. Sarah- I truly appreciate you and owe you a few dinners.

The cover design was quite a challenge. I went through several iterations, but with the feedback and help from people like Nicole Gebhardt, Amanda Moxham, Laura Jones, Audra Riddle, Jade Simmons, Tammy Imel, my mastermind group, and my Facebook feedback group- I was able to land on a final design. Thanks so much for your desire to help me.

I met a wonderful woman this year, Marshawn Evans Daniels, and her inspiring husband, Jack A. Daniels. This power-packing couple gave me just the oomph I needed to create the right messaging around my mission, which influenced my book. Thank you, dear friends, for your passion and support of me.

I would be remiss if I didn't mention my mother, Earline, who has never doubted my ability to succeed. I am humbly grateful for her attention, supportive words, and her precious life.

Finally, I want to recognize my source of strength and lifeline, JC. You have carried me through so many hard times and caused me to show up like a bright bulb in the room. It seems like yesterday that I was a single parent picking up change in the Wal-Mart parking lot so that my son Jared could attend a school activity. You brought me all the way to "Wall Street" so that I could encourage the corporate world, and help people break free from their career prisons. You made me jump off a cliff in faith in order to reach a larger audience, and you have gone above and beyond to care for my family. My life is yours completely, and I surrender all to you.